PG | Parental Guidance
Essential Tools For Conquering
7 Parenting Traps

From the Bestselling Authors of Parenting Partners
David and Patty Bunker
Illustrated by Ernie Hergenroeder

Heritage Builders
Helping You Build a Family of Faith

Table of Contents

CHAPTER 2
Hebrews 12 as the Foundation for Discipline

CHAPTER 3
The First Trap: Taking the Argument Bait

CHAPTER 4
Tool 1: Clear Expectations & Direct Communication

CHAPTER 5
Tool 2: Standing your Ground - Because You're the Parent

CHAPTER 6
Tool 3: Deflecting Arguments with the Shield

CHAPTER 7
Tool 4: Confidence in the Value of Discipline

CHAPTER 8
Tool 5: Applying Consequences

CHAPTER 9
Tool 6: Following Through and Letting Consequences Work

CHAPTER 10
Tool 7: Being the Parent, Not a Buddy

CONCLUSION
Pushing Through Every Trap and Obstacle

APPENDIX 1
Identity Destroyers and Builders

APPENDIX 2

APPENDIX 3

Table of Illustrations

APPENDIX 1

Table of Lists

Introduction

Parents Have the Power

This book is for parents who are going from "good to great" in their parenting skills. You wouldn't be reading this book if you weren't already a good parent. The parents you see on "Cops" may need some more fundamental skills than we're offering here, but they're probably not reading this. The skills presented here are prevention skills for parents who are looking for practical tools that can be put to work right away.

You've made the commitment to be your child's guide in the process of growing morally and spiritually. Sacagawea guided Lewis and Clark across the Rockies to the Pacific Ocean while carrying her newborn son. The expedition would not have succeeded without her. You are your children's Sacagawea, guiding them to success.

The authors lead a ministry that brings thousands of parents through parent leadership workshops each year. What skills are parents most interested in? Those that build structure and discipline in the home. We've found a hunger for practical skills that really create consistency in discipline. When parents give their children the gift of positive discipline, they're giving them a gift that lasts. It's the gift that provides the mental, moral, and spiritual muscle for good decision making throughout their lives.

> **This book is all about the practical. These are tools that are realistic to use, but also powerful.**

Time magazine featured a research study showing that when children develop disciplined impulse control early on, they avoid compulsive addictions like gambling later. The study followed a sample of kindergartners through sixth grade. It started by rating the kindergarteners' ability to pay attention and control their impulses. By sixth grade, many children who had difficulty paying attention in kindergarten had already started gambling behaviors like video poker. Why? Because their brains had not developed the ability to control impulses while they were young.

Children's brains develop their executive function, the ability to make good decisions, very early. "The more training the brain receives at this stage, the better it will function later in life."[1]

Parents are able to literally shape their children's brains, especially the prefrontal lobes - the decision making center - through positive discipline. As parents guide children at each stage of their development, they literally gain the mental and moral muscle to make healthy choices that will make them safer. Parents have that kind of power! Your investment in guidance and discipline is the solid gold investment you make in the success of your children. It really pays off!

Practical, Tested Tools

This book is all about the practical. We'll be presenting tools that are realistic to use, but also powerful. Before writing this book we invested fifteen years in delivering these tools to parents through our parent leadership workshops, "Parenting Partners."

During this time more than 1000 of our volunteer trainers have led parent leadership groups, taking parents through eight weeks of Parenting Partners training. They've led more than 3000 of these parent groups and developed a wealth of experience about what works in parenting. These parents come from many backgrounds and speak many languages. They are from most states and provinces in the United States and Canada, as well as Mexico and South America. These parents have moved from sometimes dreading discipline to embracing it as a great investment. This book presents the best practices and key parenting skills that developed through this process.

---

[1] Gambling, *Time* December 7, 2009, *p. 58*

Clipping Their Wings - or Giving Them Wings?

Parents can lack enthusiasm and motivation for discipline because of a feeling that discipline is negative. They may feel that discipline is controlling bad behavior and clipping their children's wings.

Controlling bad behavior certainly is one of the functions of discipline. Walk into any grocery store or Walmart and you'll probably see plenty of wings that need clipping and bad behavior that needs controlling.

Children and young people with "Discipline Deficit Disorder" will struggle to become independent adults. By contrast, discipline leads to independence and self-sufficiency.

So discipline gives them wings! It's the investment that opens up choices in life. Discipline is about building up our children, not taking away from them. Our daughter Katie demonstrated a strong personality from day one. We started thinking, "How can we preserve this strength of character and personality?" We thought about her future teen years from the time she was a baby, knowing that we wanted a strong, confident teen who would lead her peers, not be pressured by them.

> **Children and young people with "Discipline Deficit Disorder" struggle to become independent adults. By contrast, discipline leads to independence and self-sufficiency.**

Parents who have that outcome in mind are more willing to look past the little inconveniences and think about the long-term outcomes. We're willing to experience discipline ourselves to invest in our children's positive future. For example, one of our daughter's unique personality traits as a teen was that she wouldn't take medicine in pill form. Finding the same medicine in liquid form was sometimes challenging. One day we spent three hours checking pharmacies around the city to get one prescription filled as a liquid.

She felt bad, saying, "I'll bet you think I'm a real pain." We said, "No way. You have individuality. We don't have to worry about you. When other young people are abusing drugs, we know you wouldn't take pills to save your life. You're afraid of needles and you think alcohol is disgusting. We like that you have a strong personality with your own opinions and feelings." We also reminded her that her aunt didn't take pills until she was forty, and somehow managed to have a successful career working in the White House.

As it turns out, Katie successfully navigated the teenage experience, and the strength of her character and personality served her well.

Unity Among Parents

The experience of mastering these skills in discipline will unify Dads and Moms (and Grandparents and other caregivers) in their practice of discipline. You probably know families in which one parent is the disciplinarian and the other parent or caregiver works to modify or neutralize that approach. You know how much tension that can create. However, these tools and techniques are so practical that even a parent who dreads discipline can do them. It's essential that both parents commit to standing strong in practicing these discipline tools. That's equally true if parents live separately, of course.

A parent is a leader by definition and job description. A Scriptural passage in Philippians 2:1-11 reveals the essentials of leadership. Verse 4 reads "Each of you should look not only to your own interests, but to the interest of others." A parent, as a servant leader in the example of Jesus, puts the interest of their children above their own interests.

Therefore parents will work together to give their children the gift of discipline, and will sacrifice every inclination to leave their spouse hanging alone as the disciplinarian. We believe this book will provide some tools to empower parents to this level of unity.

Now we'll let you get into the practical tools in the chapters ahead, and continue on your journey of strengthening your family and your children's future.

Chapter 1

It's a Jungle Out There

Life in the Jungle

Ever since you were a kid, you've thought about how you would someday discipline your children. You've thought about how you were raised and what you would do differently.

You've thought about:

- Fairness - treating all the children in the family equally.
- Openness - listening to your children patiently and not jumping to conclusions.
- Discernment - remembering the tricks you pulled on your parents and hoping you wouldn't be so gullible when you became a parent.

You had it all figured out when you were young, and now you have your own children. So how's it going? Are you discovering some of the traps and pitfalls of parenting? Are you discovering that "it's a jungle out there"?

As you invest in the positive discipline of your children, you're making vital, essential contributions to their spiritual development.

Stories from the Jungle

Here are some real-life jungle reports Patty has heard in her work counseling families and teaching:

- Veronica is a single mom with two toddler sons and a teenage daughter, Amy. After the younger children were born, Amy changed from a straight-A student to a sullen, argumentative, distant young woman. She regularly skips school, she is failing four of her six classes, and she lies to her mother about her whereabouts on the weekend.

- Todd and Paula are parents of three young children, ages six to ten. They are running themselves ragged between two jobs, soccer practice, dance classes, and homework. Every night the children come up with new, creative arguments about why they should not go to bed, brush their teeth, or turn off the TV at the appointed time. Todd and Paula don't have enough energy for the arguments, so they find themselves giving in time after time just to keep the peace.

- José is a bright twelve-year-old boy who gets good grades, is the pitcher on his baseball team, and loves Guitar Hero. Recently he started hanging out with some older kids who smoke, disrespect the teachers, and party on the weekends. Now José thinks they are cool, but that his parents are mean and "don't have a clue" because they won't let him go to the parties. Recently, he told his parents he was spending the night with his best friend, but actually went to a party instead.

- Emma is a cute two-year-old with a sunny disposition. Her parents adore her, and they find it very hard to resist her charming ways. Emma gets pretty much everything she wants. If she doesn't, she throws an all-out temper tantrum which generally does the trick.

> **Parents love to give good gifts to their children (Matthew 7:11). So why do so many parents rob their children of the gift of positive discipline?**

- Paige, a four-year-old, has brilliant reasoning skills that can outwit her parents in every argument. Most of the time her parents laugh, thinking she's endearing and bright, but they are a little worried about the teen years!

Perhaps you've had some jungle experiences of your own that help you relate. You may already be in the thick of the jungle and need to find a way out. Well, if you're looking for some new strategies and tools, you've come to the right place! Jungle explorers have tools: maps to navigate, machetes to cut through the vines, binoculars to see ahead, ropes to cross, and lamps to see in the darkness. Here you'll find powerful parenting tools; just the gear you need to navigate through that jungle.

What is Discipline, and Why is it so Powerful?

Before we look at the traps that keep us from successful discipline for our children, let's ask, "What is discipline?"

We define discipline as:

- Training or learning that develops strong character, self-control, and moral capacity.
- Training that empowers a person to learn from mistakes and be equipped for success next time.

Discipline is the skill-set that empowers your children to fulfill their potential. It equips them to develop a growing spiritual life, to create healthy relationships, and to succeed in school and vocation. It becomes the ultimate gift from parents to children.

Let's go further by asking what is the root word connected to the word discipline? Discipline … Disciple. Discipline equips a child or young person for discipleship. As you invest in the positive discipline of your children, you're making a vital, essential contribution to their spiritual development. Discipline will empower them to be better disciples of Jesus.

You may not be able to provide your child with everything you'd like to. You may not be able to pass on all your talents and abilities. You may not be able to protect them from painful feelings or experiences. But you can give them a powerful gift for their success, now and later: positive, effective discipline.

Results from
Positive Discipline

What are the outcomes of positive discipline? Your children will be equipped for:

- Spiritual development and discipleship.
- Self-control.
- Responsibility.
- Character.
- Moral behavior.
- Learning.
- Readiness to change and improve.
- Positive identity.
- Good manners.
- Resiliency to bounce back from mistakes.
- Security and belonging (see chapter 2, on Hebrews 12).

This is just the start; you can make this list much longer.

Love and discipline are solid-gold gifts that all parents can give their children. Parents love to give good gifts to their children (Matthew 7:11). So why do so many parents rob their children of the gift of discipline?

We won't take your time to give examples of children who are shortchanged in the discipline department. We're confident that you've seen some examples lately (or if you're missing out, take a field trip to the local grocery store or Walmart). Let's just agree that too many families suffer from "Discipline Deficit Disorder"!

What are some leading causes of "Discipline Deficit Disorder"? Take a look at some of the traps parents have to overcome to avoid a discipline downfall.

The Seven Parenting Traps

◆ TRAP ONE ◆

Taking the Argument Bait

- This is the king of all parenting traps. Nothing causes parents to feel discouraged like falling into the trap of arguing. It's a real confidence buster!

- Arguments are a diabolical method of taking parents out of "the parent zone," the feeling of security and assurance that parents need. Yet children are really good at arguing. They've got skills! Fortunately, this book is all about empowering parents to build their own set of skills.

- We'll unmask this trap in Chapters 3 and 4.

◆ TRAP TWO ◆

Getting Manipulated -
Reasoning and Negotiating Everything

- Children and teens love to ensnare parents by getting them to justify and negotiate every family rule and routine, over and over. What an ambush!

- In this trap parents are pulled into justifying and negotiating everything. They're lured into feeling they need to answer to their children for all their standards, schedules, and family customs.

- We'll contend with this ploy in Chapter 5.

◆ TRAP THREE ◆

Getting Trapped by Routine Conflicts

- Parents who are enticed into arguing and negotiating too much find themselves trapped by routine conflicts. Parents can get played until they're tempted to lose their cool.

- Do you notice that most arguments are over daily routines? That it's the same argument every day or every week? You may discern that these arguments usually occur at the same time each day. What can parents do to end these cycles?

- We'll get control of this trap in Chapter 6.

◆ TRAP FOUR ◆

Confusing Discipline and Punishment

- Parents often think of setting consequences as "punishing" their children. That usually creates a tangle of mixed feelings and misgivings that hinder them from bringing discipline to their children.

- When parents feel that discipline is less than positive, they start feeling guilty about imposing discipline. How do we tell the difference between discipline and punishment? How do we discover guilt-free discipline?

- We'll disentangle parents from this trap in Chapter 7.

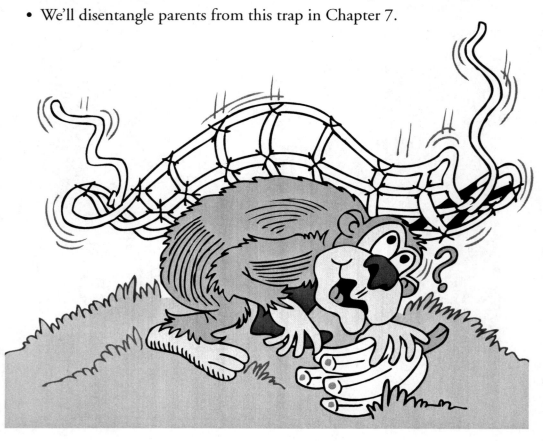

◆ TRAP FIVE ◆

Avoiding Setting Consequences

- When parents neglect consequences, their children miss out on valuable lessons and are left vulnerable. They miss out on learning from their mistakes and developing the discernment and judgment they need to become independent adults.

- How can children and teens grow without consequences? What stands in the way of parents teaching their children with consequences?

- We'll deal with this pitfall in Chapter 8.

◆ TRAP SIX ◆

Undermining Consequences/Rescuing

- Our discipline is ineffective when we don't follow through. Lack of follow-through generates stress, power struggles, loss of control, low self-esteem, and loss of confidence. It undermines discipline.

- Unless we follow through, our children will not respect us and learn to successfully handle negative influences like peer pressure, alcohol, drugs, and other risky behavior.

- We'll handle this snare in Chapter 9.

◆ TRAP SEVEN ◆

Falling for the Buddy Trap

- Who is going to give consequences to their buddies? Buddies watch each other's backs; they don't hold each other accountable and create discipline. They try to avoid consequences.

- When parents get stuck in the buddy trap, they create a permissive parenting system. Their children then miss out on the learning that occurs through discipline and consequences. Then when kids become teenagers, parents are out of options.

- We'll outwit this ambush in Chapter 10.

You may recognize most of these traps and have some of your own to add to the list. We'll learn to recognize the traps. More important, we'll take the initiative to counter the traps with the Seven Parenting Tools.

Tools for Navigating the Discipline Jungle

No matter how many traps lurk in the parenting jungle, we're not intimidated. We're not going to back away from the adventure of parenting. We have our own jungle camp filled with powerful tools. We have a team to pursue this adventure together.

We can pick up our tools: maps to navigate, machetes to cut through the vines, binoculars to see ahead, ropes for crossings, and lamps to see in the darkness. Take a look at seven parenting tools that can be in every parent's camp.

No matter how many traps lurk in the parenting jungle, we're not intimidated.

The Seven Parenting Tools

◆ TOOL ONE ◆

Clear Expectations and Direct Communication

- Just as jungle commanders give clear orders in battle, parents lead their families by creating clear expectations and instructions. This tool will equip parents with some simple techniques for giving their children directions.

- The practical "Clear Expectations" tool uses the five points of "Who, What, When, Where, and How Often" for parents to clearly communicate with their children. This results in more work getting done and fewer arguments getting started.

- Get going with this tool in Chapter 4.

◆ TOOL TWO ◆

Standing Your Ground: Because You're the Parent

- In navigating the jungle, you have to find the high ground and hold it. This tool empowers parents with the confidence to simply and effortlessly stand their ground.

- Parents can develop family rules and routines that include the parents' own preferences and personalities. They don't need to negotiate away their own needs and boundaries, or feel guilty about valuing their own personality. When we respect ourselves and teach our children to respect us, we're giving them the essentials for their social and moral development.

- Check out this tool in Chapter 5.

◆ TOOL THREE ◆

Deflecting Arguments with The Shield

- If you have time to master just one Parenting Tool, this is the one! With the Shield, you'll GIT-R-DONE! That is, you'll get your children to do what you instruct, without any fuss or muss. The old days of getting trapped in arguments will be gone.
- The Shield is a real game changer because it ends habits and patterns of arguments. This tool empowers parents to feel the confidence that we call "the Parent Zone."
- Practice the Shield in Chapter 6.

◆ TOOL FOUR ◆

Confidence in the Value of Positive Discipline

- This tool will strengthen parents' confidence in discipline and transform it from an exhausting ordeal to a simple, natural interaction. This is guilt-free parenting.
- Children gain the essentials for success from positive discipline, including responsibility, self-control, positive self-identity and resiliency. Here's where they gain the power to learn from their mistakes, bounce back from disappointments, and find guidance from their parents.
- Gear up for this tool in Chapter 7.

◆ TOOL FIVE ◆

Applying Consequences

- Consequences are the weight room of moral development. These are the training tools that give children the mental and moral capacity to develop positive action and habits.

- With consequences, parents can bring on the fun, drama, and creativity. Consequences are learning tools, and parents love to teach. Because we are calm and in control, parents can really have fun with consequences.
- Get outfitted with this tool in Chapter 8.

◆ TOOL SIX ◆

Following Through and Letting Consequences Work

- Follow-though creates consistency. Consistency makes us authentic and credible. Credibility results in respect. Children will model their behavior after those they respect.
- Children and teens respond to action. They don't usually respond to words unless they know their parents will take action.
- Operate this tool in Chapter 9.

◆ TOOL SEVEN ◆

Being the Parent, Not a Buddy

- Parents have two choices: Be the parent now and the buddy later. Or be the buddy now and the parent forever. When parents discipline their children as they grow, their children gain the skills and confidence to become independent young adults.

- This tool will focus on how parents can make the "Six Adjustments for Parents of Teens." Teenage is the time for parents to step up their support. Parents can really be there when their sons and daughters need them the most.

- Get equipped with this tool in Chapter 10.

You may already be an expert with some of these tools, but you'll get fully powered up with all your parenting tools for positive discipline with these chapters.

Are You Ready?

Are you ready for some adventure? After training parents with these skills, we often ask children if they notice any changes at home. Their faces light up! They feel so much more secure and settled as their parents practice these skills. Their confidence in their future grows. We even hear from their teachers, who report that these children and young people are finding more success in school. It takes some effort to navigate the parenting jungle, but it's worth it!

SEVEN PARENTING TRAPS & TOOLS

TRAPS	TOOLS	CHAPTER NO.
Taking the Argument Bait	Clear Expectations & Direct Communication	3 and 4
Getting Manipulated: Reasoning & Negotiating Everything	Standing Your Ground: Because You're the Parent	5
Getting Trapped by Routine Conflicts	Deflecting Arguments with the Shield	6
Confusing Discipline & Punishment	Confidence in the Value of Positive Discipline	7
Avoiding Setting Consequences	Applying Consequences	8
Undermining Consequences/Rescuing	Following Through & Letting Consequences Work	9
Falling for the Buddy Trap	Being the Parent, Not a Buddy	10

Chapter 2

Hebrews 12 as the Foundation for Discipline

Starting with a Solid Foundation

Parents know that children and teens need a strong sense of security and belonging in order to form a positive self-identity. Parents take that responsibility to heart. With a task so crucial, we need a solid foundation for understanding how discipline can produce these outcomes.

Years ago, the authors discovered a foundational source for the power of positive discipline in Hebrews 12:7-11. We want to start with this passage because it shaped our view of discipline. The purpose of the Seven Parenting Tools found in this book is to put these biblical principles into action.

Positive Discipline Creates Positive Identity

Hebrews 12:8 says: *If you are not disciplined (and everyone undergoes discipline), then you are illegitimate children and not true sons.*

Doesn't that lay it on the line? Could anything be more direct?

When parents give the gift of discipline, children know that they genuinely belong in the family. When children don't receive the gift of discipline, they wonder if the family even wants them. They may question whether their family values them at all.

Positive Discipline Creates Security and Self-Worth

What picture does this passage create in your mind? Can you see how positive discipline creates a den of security and belonging?

A wonderful illustration of Hebrews 12:8 occurred in Patty's family. She is the first of four children, and her brother Rowland is the youngest. When he was in elementary school, their parents died, so he needed a family to live with. A family in his church shared a similar background with his family, and they immediately took him in. They had two sons older than Rowland.

Now, wouldn't it have been natural for the new family to say, "Rowland, don't worry about doing your homework, you've been through so much?"

"Hey, Rowland, you don't need to do chores like everyone else, because you're having a hard time."

And, "You're the youngest of both families."

And, "You just got here."

Would he have been happy with that? He would have loved it - he was twelve! *Party on, dude - I can do whatever I want!* All his friends would have envied him. But, as you can imagine, his family did the right thing. They treated him like their other two sons by raising him with positive discipline. It wasn't two sons plus honored visitor.

> **Children deprived of discipline take it personally.**

It was three sons. They became his brothers and parents. That relationship became solid and permanent.

Rowland is now a successful father himself. He's the chief financial officer in an international company. You can count on him. His family gave him the gifts of discipline and belonging that gave him the capacity to be a great dad and successful man.

Building Positive Identity

Nothing could be less compassionate or loving than depriving your children of discipline. What if Rowland's family had treated him like a hotel guest instead of a son? Sure, he would have enjoyed it at the time - but eventually he would have felt left out of the family. Excluded. Rejected.

Children deprived of discipline take it personally. They take it to heart. They feel as if nobody cares, that they're just not worth it, and that they don't fit in. The sense of security and self-worth that comes with being treated like a son or daughter, rather than a guest, builds positive self-identity.

Now, will your children or teens say, "Thanks, Dad, for making me mow the lawn, do my homework, and practice music"? Not a chance! They won't be happy about that at all. Nevertheless, as parents we practice leadership and do the right thing by raising our children with positive discipline. We don't worry about the popularity polls because we know that we are giving our children a great gift.

Discipline Produces Righteousness and Peace

Hebrews 12:11 says: *No discipline seems pleasant at the time, but painful. Later on, however, it produces a harvest of righteousness and peace for those who have been trained by it.*

Look at the illustration in Chapter 7, "Discipline is Practice for Success." It's helpful to think about whether our children would be happy if they only did what was enjoyable. Playing in the ball game on Saturday is fun, but why waste time going to practice during the week? Who really needs to run laps and practice drills? You may hear your children saying, "Why do I need to study … go to practice … sit down at the piano?" Yet you know that without practice they wouldn't enjoy the game or performance, and they'd be humiliated on the field, at the performance, and at school.

Children who are raised in a family with no structure, little communication, and vague expectations may enjoy getting their own way and be envied by their friends, but they're unlikely to feel secure or cared for. No doubt, discipline is unpleasant, inconvenient, and just plain painful. But is there any other way to success?

Our Hopes and Dreams for Our Children

We've listened to thousands of parents tell us their hopes and dreams for their children as they grow up. In almost every parent group, wherever they are, they list:

- To love God.
- To be responsible citizens and productive members of society.
- To go to college.
- To have good jobs.
- To be good role models for their peers.
- To become independent adults.

Which of these goals can be accomplished without discipline that seems difficult or painful at the time? Obviously, none of them. Which of these goals represents a harvest of righteousness and peace? Certainly every one of them.

Parents Invest in Discipline for Their Children's Success

It's interesting to notice that as parents we not only train our children to be disciplined, but we also take the same path of discipline ourselves. Is administering discipline pleasant at the time, or is it painful? Is it pleasant to take our children to one more music lesson or sports practice? Is it pleasant to follow through with consequences when they misbehave?

> **Discipline is the essential investment that allows our children to become independent and responsible.**

Patty and her siblings all played stringed instruments. David's father taught his children woodwinds. Was it pleasant or was it painful for the parents to listen to their children's squeaking violins and saxophones? The harvest of peace came later. Much, much later. Are we willing to make that investment for our children? Are dads and moms willing to discipline in unity, even if they are separated or divorced? Are we willing to risk a plunge in the popularity polls with our teens and kids?

Discipline is the essential investment that allows our children to become independent and responsible. Can you imagine why any parent would shortchange their children of this gift?

There is a wildly extreme example of parents who keep their children in a dependent state: Munchausen syndrome by proxy (MSBP). In MSBP a parent sabotages a child's health in order to create attention for the parent. Such parents literally poison their children to keep them in the home or hospital.

The movie *The Sixth Sense* features two sisters victimized by this kind of parent.

This MSBP disorder is rare, bizarre, and disturbing. But aren't parents who withhold discipline from their children sabotaging them and keeping their children from reaching their goals and potential?

Equipping Our Children to Understand Hardship

Consider the extended passage in Hebrews 12:7 - 11: *Endure hardship as discipline; God is treating you as sons. For what son is not disciplined by his father? If you are not disciplined (and everyone undergoes discipline), then you are illegitimate children and not true sons. Moreover, we have all had human fathers who disciplined us and we respected them for it. How much more should we submit to the Father of our spirits and live! Our fathers disciplined us for a little while as they thought best; but God disciplines us for our good, that we may share in his holiness. No discipline seems pleasant at the time, but painful. Later on, however, it produces a harvest of righteousness and peace for those who have been trained by it.*

When we look at the Scripture in Hebrews 12, we recognize that it's speaking to our relationship with God. We may experience illness, disability, or accidents. We may suffer betrayal by friends or loved ones. We may deal with the stress of jobs that require too many hours and provide too little income.

How do we regard our suffering? Is God showing contempt for us, giving us what we deserve? This Scripture teaches quite the opposite: our trials are experiences of discipline proving that we belong to God. As we raise our children with a system of positive discipline, we are preparing our children for a positive, intimate relationship with their heavenly Father.

Why Not Me?

We have a friend who experienced the loss of both his father and brother within the space of a few weeks. He felt overwhelmed, and wondered when he would come out of the tunnel of grief. He found himself continually asking himself, "Why me?" Then a strange thought came to him, prompting him to wonder, "Why not me?"

He started thinking, "Why shouldn't I walk with Jesus, 'A Man of Sorrows,' and familiar with suffering" (Isaiah 53:3). He came to view his ongoing experiences with suffering as a gift. As a pastor and counselor, he's now shared that gift with countless others who are walking through experiences of loss and affliction.

One of the authors, David, faced a similar situation of "Why not me?" Just before high school graduation I developed an autoimmune disease that produced a catalog of painful symptoms such as arthritis. The disease continued into my twenties and thirties. After all those years, I was referred to Stanford University's Medical School to be treated by the distinguished rheumatologist, Dr. Halsted Holman.

When children experience the loving discipline of parents, then they learn to interpret hardship in life as being a sign of belonging, not rejection.

Dr. Homan entered the examination room and said, "You've had this disease longer than anyone. Therefore I'm going to make you an expert in this disease so that you can teach my residents about it during rounds." He then opened up a writing board and taught me about the condition in depth so that I could then explain it to his students.

By putting me to work right away, Dr. Holman didn't give me a chance to feel sorry for myself. He didn't let me dwell on the revelation that I'd had the condition longer than anyone. I'd always wanted to win something, but I was thinking of something more like the Daytona 500, not the "Best in Disease" award. However, the Hebrews 12:7, "Endure hardship as discipline; God is treating you as sons" passage prepared me for taking on the "why not me" attitude. Dr. Holman's empowering approach reinforced the dignity of finding purpose out of the pain.

About the same time, when Patty and I were starting a ministry to parents, and Dr. Holman's approach strongly influenced our approach. Instead of bringing information and services to parents, we took a leadership approach of equipping parents to become greatly skilled so they could train others. We realized that people master what they teach, and that they need the dignity of giving to others. This approach set the stage for reaching thousands of parents across countless cultures.

As parents raise children with the gift of positive discipline, their children are equipped to face hardship with a "Why not me" approach; they're empowered to create gifts from suffering.

Preparing Our Children to Understand Love

When we train our children with discipline, we're giving them the experience they need to understand love. When we lead our children through difficult experiences, such as when they apologize to a teacher because they cheated on a test, we're modeling to them our belief that they're worth it - they are people of great value.

Without this example of loving discipline, children can grow up to feel rejected by God if they experience anything short of winning the lottery on a regular basis. When children experience the loving discipline of parents, then they learn to interpret *hardship* in life as being a sign of belonging, not rejection. If we can give them only one capacity for their spiritual development, it should be to understand that God loves them and values them *when they experience adversity!* Then they will be equipped for spiritual growth.

With this foundation for the vital role of discipline, let's find and disarm the parenting traps that try to sabotage our children's futures.

Chapter 3

The First Trap:
Taking the Argument Bait

The King of the Traps

The king of the parenting traps is Taking the Argument Bait. This is the Tiger Trap, Cage Trap, Net Trap, Monkey Trap, and Stake Pit Trap all rolled into one. Nothing causes parents to feel discouraged like getting entangled in arguments with their children. Arguments are the most effective way of taking parents out of "the parent zone," the feeling of confidence and purpose that parents need.

> **As much as you might want to reason with your child during an argument, by definition, it is not going to work!**

Because this trap is so important, we're giving it its own chapter. But we'll follow with three chapters presenting three powerful parenting tools that will disarm this trap. With these tools, parents can be free from participating in pointless arguments with their children. But even in this chapter, parents will learn practical ways to identify and avoid power struggles.

Taking the Argument Bait

Our children can be very creative at arguing with us, even over the simplest instructions. Often the arguments are about routine, everyday things such as setting the table for dinner. We find ourselves spending a great deal of energy floundering in the trap our children have set for us. Whenever we argue with our children, we've taken the bait.

- How many times have you found yourself arguing with your child over the simplest instruction?

- What happened? Did you feel like you won the argument?

- When you get trapped into an argument with your children, how do you end up feeling?

When we ask this in our groups, most parents say, "It always feels bad." Our children are geniuses at arguments. They practice all day long with their friends. Have you watched little children negotiating the rules of a ball game or teens discussing their weekend plans? They've got skills! How about your children? How are their skills in debating, negotiating, and arguing?

We're happy that our children can debate and hold their own with their peers. Most of our kids could go straight to law school; they really know how to argue! The question is - why on earth would you want to compete against those skills?

Why is it Important Not to Argue with Your Children?

Because you can't win. Your children will always win! Even if you think you can match your child's reasoning and debating skills (which you can't, because they're argument geniuses), you would still lose. Why? Take a look at the upcoming section under the heading Five Reasons Why Kids and Teens Argue, and you'll see that you're just getting played.

Our young children are great arguers, just like older children, aren't they? A parent in one of our Parenting Partners groups told us about her frustration with her preschooler. This parent is a teacher who picks up her preschooler every afternoon and drives home. During the drive, her daughter inevitably starts a discussion about dinner. The parent describes the dinner she's planning at home, and

> **It's important for us to realize that as long as we are arguing with our children, we are no longer leading our family. If we're not leading, they're not growing.**

her daughter immediately suggests they go to McDonald's or Taco Bell instead. The mother starts giving reasons why the home-cooked dinner is better, and her daughter counters with reasons why fast food is superior.

Sounds Like an Argument to Me

How do you know that this is an argument and not just a discussion of feelings and opinions? Because her daughter initiates the same conversation every day. Always at the same time, and always on the same subject. How do you know that this is an argument? Because until recently the mother felt frustrated that she took the bait day after day and always felt manipulated. What's more, she felt annoyed and angry.

She knew her daughter was pushing her buttons but didn't know what to do about it. The good news is that she applied *The Shield* technique (coming up in Chapter 6), and it worked perfectly. Their conversations are now pleasant, not irritating, and the mother has become much more confident and settled in her parenting ability.

Arguing: It Just Doesn't Work

Let's look at why we should not argue. We define an argument as "a challenge of the will." It is not a discussion, a negotiation, or an attempt to arrange a meeting of the minds. Therefore, as much as you might want to reason with your child during an argument, by definition, it is not going to work!

Arguing with our children is like putting our finger in a Finger Trap. Have you tried this exercise in futility lately? The Trap is a device made of braided paper. Two people insert their index fingers and pull against each other. As they pull, the trap tightens. How do they get free from the finger trap? They push their fingers together, and the trap opens up.

Parents experience the same futility during arguments. The parent pulls against the child by trying to reason and negotiate, and both get trapped.

Five Reasons
Why Kids and Teens Argue

There are at least five reasons why children argue with their parents. What do you think those reasons might be?

Here are some of our favorites:

1. To avoid or delay doing the task.

- As long as children argue, they successfully avoid doing the task we've asked them to do.

- Even if they eventually do the task, they have manipulated their parents by doing it when they please. Aren't parents setting up future conflicts by teaching them to disregard instructions and delay doing a task?

2. To wear out parents until they give up.

- Children often will argue relentlessly until parents give in out of frustration or exhaustion. If children know this has worked in the past, they will be amazingly persistent in this phase.

- Parents lose confidence and feel drained when they have to bargain every time they need their children to comply with instructions. Children are energized by wheeling and dealing, but it wears down the batteries of parents.

3. To distract parents from their instructions.

- If your children can trap you into an argument, they've created the distraction they need to avoid or delay following your instructions. In an argument your children may storm out in anger, or you may send them somewhere else to calm down. If so, the diversion worked.

- Do you remember test days when you were in school? Did you or your classmates suddenly come up with riveting questions to engage your teacher, trying craftily to distract her from starting the test? Or perhaps you created excuses and other negotiating tactics. It's all part of the game, so watch out for your children's diversionary tactics. Don't get played!

4. To have fun and be entertained.

- Children sometimes try to get their parents confused and upset just for the sheer entertainment of it. It's fun to push Mom's or Dad's buttons and watch us dance!

5. To have the control and power.

- If children succeed through arguing - if they can draw Mom and Dad into an argument and divert, delay, or dissolve Mom's and Dad's instructions - they are in control of how the family functions.

- Even though children may enjoy running the ship, ultimately they feel more secure when parents stay at the helm as the ship's captain.

Can you see that when we argue with our children, they are in control, and we are not? Does that surprise you?

Take a look at the illustration "Why Do Kids Argue?" Here we see that the reason kids argue is "Because they want control!" They want to be in charge.

It's important for us to realize that as long as we are arguing with our children, we are no longer leading our family. If we're not leading, they're not growing. Only when parents are leading can children and young people receive the support and guidance they need.

We give our children the gift of discipline as the resource for their future success. If we show them that arguing is an acceptable way to dominate a relationship, we're undermining their ability to have healthy, intimate relationships in the future. We need give them an alternative to that pattern, replacing that bad habit with more positive ways of relating.

> **In an argument, your child holds all the aces.**

What Happens in Your Home?

Think about the arguments in your home. Which of these five reasons do you experience with your children? Now these aren't the only reasons why kids and teens argue. What are some of the creative reasons your children argue?

Earlier we mentioned that an argument can be defined as "a challenge of the will." It is not a discussion, a negotiation, or an attempt to arrange a meeting of the minds. Do you disagree? Well, you're wrong. Just kidding! But notice that there is a difference between arguments and discussions.

Arguments vs. Discussions

There's nothing negative about children expressing their feelings, opinions, and thoughts. It's okay to have debates with parents. When our daughter hit middle school, she started using dinnertime to practice her debating skills, taking the opposite side on most discussions. Her dad remarked, "You're really good at debating. I bet you'd do well in forensics in high school." Sure enough, she did forensics in high school and won her tournaments from the start.

Our children practice their reasoning and debating skills in the family, and they work on finding their own voice. That's great! We want them to reason well and be able to persuade others to their point of view. So discussion and debating are positive tools in our child's development. But what about arguments?

If parents take the bait and argue, they become trapped and give up leadership.

In an argument, your child holds all the aces. When David was a high school freshman, the seniors invited him to a Friday night poker game. At first feeling flattered by being included, he soon realized that it was a setup. The seniors were working together to cheat. Well, when it comes to arguments, your children are the seniors, and you're the freshman who's been bamboozled.

How do you Know
When it's an Argument?

- **There's work to be done.** It's time to do homework, walk the dog, do the dishes, or meet a curfew. When's there's a task at hand and you see the "Five Reasons Kids and Teens Argue" kicking in - you know the trap is set.

- **Look at the clock.** Do you notice that most arguments happen at the same time of day? Usually right when you get home or after dinner. Why? Because your kids have the advantage: you're bone tired, and they're wound up. That's not a discussion, that's an ambush.

- **Your intuition kicks in.** You've seen the Westerns in which the gang of outlaws makes the good guy "dance" by shooting at his feet? Well then, you know the feeling when you're being played and trapped by arguments.

We've looked at why children and teens argue. Let's now take a look at their playbook and see how they do it.

The Left Side of the Volcano:
How Young People Argue

As you look at "The Erupting Volcano" illustration, you see a picture of how conflict builds between the child and the parent. See if you recognize some of the common ways that children argue with parents on the left side of the volcano.

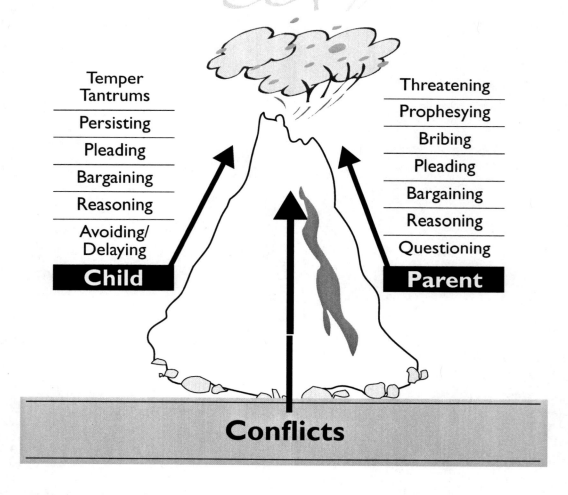

Screaming Put Downs Yelling
Hitting Throwing Things
Exploding in Anger

Temper Tantrums
Persisting
Pleading
Bargaining
Reasoning
Avoiding/ Delaying
Child

Threatening
Prophesying
Bribing
Pleading
Bargaining
Reasoning
Questioning
Parent

Conflicts

◆ Avoiding and Delaying ◆

Our children and teens can be masters of the art of delay to avoid getting to the tasks we have for them.

- "I want to play videos now. I'll finish my science project on Saturday."
- "I'll get to the dishes right after this show is done."
- "I'll feed the dog after the game."

◆ Reasoning ◆

Our children could be lawyers - they never run out of reasons for avoiding an unwanted task.

- "But it's not my turn to do the dishes; it's my sister's turn."
- "If I clean my room now, I'll never get my homework done."
- "Why should I make my science project so perfect? Everyone else just spend a few minutes on theirs."

◆ Bargaining ◆

Children often turn the reasoning into negotiating.

- "I promise I'll clean the bathroom and the kitchen next week if you'll do it for me just this once."
- "I know the curfew is 10:00, but if you let me stay at the party late, I won't ask you for a favor again."

◆ Pleading ◆

Our children can put on their most irresistible expressions when they want something.

- "Pleeease, can't I just stay up another half hour?"
- "The only thing I want for my birthday is that new phone. I'll be happy if you'll just get it for me."
- "Why can't I can't have that video game? All my other friends play it."

◆ Persisting ◆

After we think we've worn down our children's resolve to argue, they pop up again like gophers. When we allow them to argue with us, they will continue. Remember the Reasons Why Kids and Teens Argue.

- "Come on, it's not fair. No one else's parents make them go to bed this early."
- "I can't believe you're making me go to my sister's recital. You know I'll be bored."

◆ Temper Tantrums ◆

As the arguing wears on, children may add some drama to the mix. Those demonstrations may include yelling, slamming doors, stomping out, and so on.

Children engage in many different routines during an argument. What are some of your children's common routines for arguing? These are designed to avoid the task, gain power or control, or make the parent give up. If parents take the bait and argue, they become trapped and give up leadership.

The Right Side of the Volcano:
How Parents Argue

As you look at the Erupting Volcano illustration, you have a very good picture of what happens during an argument. Parents begin by telling children to do something. As children engage in various delay and control tactics, parents often reacts in one or several of the ways listed on the right side of the volcano.

Do parents need to be reasonable by their children's standards?

What are some the typical comebacks parents make to their children? As you look at these responses, notice that they are reactions to the methods that children or teens have initiated. They are not the methods of communication parents use when they are in control and leading.

◆ Questioning ◆

Questioning is when parents ask questions as a way of reasoning with the child instead of simply repeating their instructions.

- "How many times do I have to tell you?"
- "What am I going to do with you?"
- "Do you think I'm your personal maid?"
- "Why don't you ever listen to me?"

The problem is that when we ask children these questions, it gives them all the power. For example, if I have to ask my child what I should do with her or him, it certainly indicates that I don't have a plan!

Of course, these are rhetorical questions, so if the child answers any of them, then they're really in trouble.

◆ Reasoning ◆

Reasoning with your children is different than explaining the task you want done and why. Reasoning is trying to convince them to do something that you should not have to convince them to do (for instance, it is a regular expectation of your household).

Have you ever heard this kind of monologue?

"I've talked to you about TV and your homework until I'm blue in the face. And you have homework tonight. Are you doing it? No! You're watching TV night after night. Where is television ever going to get you? It won't get you a job. It won't get you into college."

Have you heard yourself talking like this and wondered, "Who am I? Where did I come up with this material?" It can feel like an out-of-body experience. Then you realize you've been trapped by reasoning.

Do parents need to be reasonable by their children's standards? I may be the only parent on the block to deny my child "Grand Theft Auto." Or so he says. I may be the only one to plan family dinners. That's okay - my children will just have to live with my eccentricities. (See more in Chapter 5.)

Remember that an argument is about a battle of the wills. This is not a reasonable discussion or dialogue. Trying to convince your child during an argument that you have good reasons for what you are asking them to do only shows them that you are not in control!

◆ Bargaining ◆

In some families, parents negotiate every instruction.

- "If you'll just finish your homework without arguing anymore, I'll let you watch that show."
- "Okay, I'll let you stay late at the party, but you'd better not ask me again."

These parents then have to walk a gauntlet of haggling, dickering, and dealing before their children will do simple tasks like homework or cleaning their room. The family practically becomes a union/management relationship. This negotiating is exhausting, and parents will either give up or blow up.

◆ Pleading ◆

Parents may begin pleading with the child when he does not immediately do what he's instructed.

- "Please try to behave just this once."
- "Come on, I'm only asking for a little cooperation. You can see that the room is a mess."
- "Don't embarrass me in front of everyone in the store."

The problem is that when we have to plead our case, we are noticeably not in control.

◆ Bribing ◆

Bribing is promising our children some kind of prize or deal in exchange for their compliance.

- "If you stop throwing a fit, I'll buy you the toy."
- "If you turn off the TV and do your homework, you won't have to do the dishes."
- "I'll let you have a piece of candy if you'll just pick up all your toys."
- "I won't tell your father if you get it done now."

The problem is that if we have to bribe our children to get them to stop unwanted behaviors, who is in control? When we resort to bribing our children to follow simple instructions, we are setting a terrible example of giving children all the power.

Of course, there is a difference between bribing our children to get them to perform simple, everyday, routine tasks and rewarding our children for extraordinary things, such as chores over and above the expected, auditioning for a play when they are very nervous, and so on. Let's think about the difference:

- A *bribe* is offered in the course of arguing and negotiating.
- A prospective *reward* is used as a positive incentive; therefore, it must be set before a request.

As you can see by the responses on the child's side of our volcano, none of these attempts on the part of the parent to control the child's behavior are working. The conflict is only escalating. Here are some more examples:

◆ Prophesying ◆

Prophesying is making predictions that even the child knows will never come true.

- "At this rate, you'll be grounded forever!"
- "If you don't do something about your horrible manners, no one will ever invite you anywhere!"
- "You'd better get your act together, or you're going to wind up a good-for-nothing like your Uncle John."
- "If you don't study this minute, you'll never make it to college."

The problem is that these kinds of predictions are so outrageous the child knows they aren't true. Or they are so far in the future she just doesn't care. An older child may take this as a dare and live up to it to spite you.

◆ Threatening ◆

Threats are different than warning the child that a consequence is about to be given. A threat is telling the child something is going to happen but failing to follow through when the behavior continues.

- "If you don't settle down, we're leaving the store."
- "Next time you do that, you're in trouble!"
- "If you do that again, you'll wish you didn't live here."
- "Just wait until your father gets home."

The problem is that when we threaten a lot without following through, children learn we don't mean what we say.

Now I'm Just Mad!

Parents use these techniques out of heartfelt motives. They're trying to reach their children in reasonable ways. However, parents need to evaluate the effectiveness of these techniques - how well do they work? Think about the results in your home - how successful are these approaches?

Most parents tell us that these well-intentioned techniques backfire, resulting in tremendous frustration. Why? It seems that the children are leading the process, and parents are reacting. In this process parents are automatically on the defensive, so it's just not going to work. The resulting frustration can be explosive.

What are some examples of exploding actions that you may see in your home, either from children, teens, or parents? On the volcano illustration you find:

- Screaming, Put-Downs, Yelling.
- Hitting, Throwing Things.
- Exploding in Anger.

How do Children React in an Argument?

When a discussion escalates into an argument, how do children react? Children or teens often respond with reflexive actions like:

- Yelling.
- Slamming doors.
- Throwing temper tantrums.
- Crying.
- Saying, "You're mean," "I hate you," etc.

What Routines do Parents Use When they Explode?

When our children explode in aggravation, how do parents react? Sometimes parents yield to frustration:

- Yelling.
- Laying on guilt trips ("you're ungrateful," "you're trying to upset me," etc.).
- Putting their children down with belittling comments.
- Becoming sarcastic.

When parents respond this way, they often think, "Where did that come from? That sounded like someone else talking - I can't believe I said that." Arguing can create an atmosphere that pulls us away from our true selves and values. It can create a sideshow where we're doing things we dislike and saying things we don't actually believe. When we get manipulated into arguing, old family scripts sometimes seem to take over.

Why do parents sometimes explode? Because we feel we can no longer manage the situation. If we think we are losing a battle, we tend to go to extremes in order to win. When we argue, we create anxiety and stress in ourselves and in our children, and the situation often escalates into an angry and out-of-control blowup.

What Happens When Arguments Stop?

Parents in our workshops tell us that when they apply the Seven Parenting Tools, they stop getting pulled into arguments so often. They report that the biggest change in their family is that yelling stops and the family becomes more peaceful.

> **When we don't get drawn into an argument, we are teaching them habits they need for successful relationships in the future. We're creating family practices and patterns that will bless our children and their children.**

That's huge, because even adults can't stand to be yelled at. For most of us that becomes a relationship breaker. If someone yells at us in a business relationship or friendship, we usually avoid working with that person or seeing them again. If it's a boss or relative that we're stuck with, we become guarded.

Try to imagine what being yelled at feels like to children who are looking to a parent for guidance, validity, and safety. They can't avoid the parent, so they have to develop coping strategies. However, as parents, we don't have to put our children in that position. We have effective strategies that can replace the futile techniques found in the Volcano.

Parenting Tools That Beat the Argument Trap

Thankfully, this is the only chapter that just focuses on a parenting trap! Now the next chapters provide parenting tools that can put an end to old traditions of spiraling arguments and put parents decisively into leadership.

You've probably heard the saying, "Do as I say, not as I do." Children learn how to act, and particularly how to handle conflict, by watching what we do. When we stay in control and don't get drawn into an argument, we are teaching them habits they need for successful relationships in the future. We're creating family practices and patterns that will bless our children and their children.

Chapter 4

Parenting Tool #1: Clear Expectations and Direct Communication

Preventing Arguments Through Clear Expectations

What gets parents off track from discipline? Getting pulled into the trap of arguing! Our children know that, as in football, the best defense is a good offense. They go on the offensive to get us off track with the goal of avoiding the tasks they need to do.

> **When you're giving instructions, it's natural to explain yourself. However, offering explanations derails the flow of instructions.**

Parents also need a good offense to get ahead of the game. This chapter gets that game plan started. The good news is that, while powerful, these tools are simple and can be mastered quickly. Our first tool is **Clear Expectations and Direct Communication.**

The Problem with Indirect Instructions

How many times have you started to correct your child for failing to follow your instructions, and then you realized that your child did not really understand the instructions?

Here's an example. Have any of you ever had this problem?

- You have a room full of children, and you say, "Okay, everybody, it's time to clean up."

- What happens?
- No one moves.

Why?

Everyone assumes you are not talking to him or her, since you have not been specific about whom you are addressing and what you expect. This will be true for most young children, teenagers, and even adults. It is simply human nature.

The Five Points of Direct Communication

Look at the illustration "Clear Expectations and Direct Communication."

Motivating our children to follow our instructions begins with giving clear expectations through direct communication. Our recommended strategy is to cover these five points:

◆ Who ◆

Say your child's name so there is no confusion about whom you are addressing.

- Leticia, turn off the TV.

◆ What ◆

Instructions should be specific and detailed. Describe what you want done.

Start with words that motivate to action, such as "stop," "take," "make," or "pick up."

- Pick your clothes up off the floor.
- Put all dirty clothes in the laundry basket.
- Fold all your clean clothes, and put them in your dresser.
- Put all the trash in the trash basket.
- Stop jumping on the couch, and sit down!

◆ When ◆

Tell your child when you want something done.

- Now!
- Before you watch TV.
- By Saturday at noon.
- Immediately after school tomorrow.

✦ Where ✦

Be specific about where you want them to be and where you expect them to put things.

- Play only in the front yard.
- Take the sheets off your bed, and put them in the laundry room in the green basket.
- Stop jumping on the sofa, and put your feet on the floor.

✦ How Often ✦

This is another helpful detail that makes expectations clear.

- Every Saturday.
- Every day.
- Every night.
- Just this once.

✦ Putting It All Together ✦

- Leticia, pick up your clothes from the floor now, and put them in the laundry room basket. Do this every night before you go to bed."

- "Michael, clear the dishes off the table now, and put them in the sink. Do this after dinner tonight and after dinner every night."

◆ Five Fingers ◆

A memory device to remember the five steps is using five fingers (the five steps of Who, What, When, Where, How Often).

Do you think these five points will help? Can you think of a current home situation in which this could help out?

◆ Charts ◆

Charts are a great tool for the five points of Clear Expectations. You may have your charts ready to go, or you can find some templates for charts on a website. We like the charts from Chart Jungle at **www.chartjungle.com**.

Practice with Your Own Home Situations

Think of some real-life situations in your family that would benefit from giving clear instructions. Try practicing with them by applying Who, What, When, Where, and How Often.

You may use these examples to get started:

- Your child is always rushed in the morning before school; she can't find her homework, shoes, and so on.

  Practice: Tell her specifically what to do to get ready the night before.

- Your daughter leaves the bathroom a mess after taking a shower and putting on her makeup.

  Practice: Tell her what to pick up, where to put it, and when to do it.

- Your teenagers don't give you enough information about where they will be after school and with whom.

  Practice: Instruct them on exactly what information you want, how and where you want it, and when you want it.

Where's the "Why"?

As you heard the five points of Clear Expectations: Who, What, When, Where, and - what were you expecting next? Probably "Why"? But we omitted why. Why?

When you're in the flow of giving instructions, it's natural to explain yourself. However, offering explanations derails the flow of instructions in several ways:

- The five points of instructions aim toward action. If the instruction is "Jeremy, please put the Toyota in the garage now and every time you get home from school," Jeremy knows what you want. He knows that if he negotiates by saying, "But Mom, I'm already starting my homework," then he's delaying or avoiding.

- However, if you explain, you interrupt the action. You actually open the door to delay and argument. Every reason invites a discussion. That's what reasoning is all about. "Jeremy, please put the Toyota in the garage now because it's about to rain," invites, "Just let me finish Twittering first, because it's not raining yet."

- When you're giving instructions and you start explaining reasons, children and especially teens often feel that you're frustrated or angry, even though you're not. Why? Check out chapter 10, where we write about teenage brain development and emotional perceptions.

- Most of the time when we give instructions, these directions are well-known by now. They guide our children through routines they are already familiar with - but which they forgot, became distracted from, or are avoiding. Our instructions are intended to get them back on track.

Then When is it Time for the "Why"?

There are definitely times when it is appropriate to reason through why a child needs to do something. When should we do that?

1. When it involves a moral issue.

Seize teaching moments around moral issues. These are so important because you are building your children's moral development. We'll discuss moral development of children in the next chapter.

Parents love to seize teaching moments around moral issues.

When the issues are everyday routines like your choice of bedtimes or curfew, don't treat these as moral issues. Don't feel obligated to reason through them like you do with moral issues. This becomes Parent Trap #2, which we will address with Parenting Tool #2 in the next chapter.

2. When you have time for a conversation.

If you're going to start a reasoning process, you should allow time for a response and conversation. Try discussing these important issues when you have unhurried time, like while driving home together or over dinner.

Say you're discussing the importance of completing the science fair assignment, or why your son can't have his girlfriend visit his room. Since these are important topics that will prompt opinions and feelings from your child, allow time for the discussion. If not, you will come across as uncaring and angry. Don't let yourself fall into that trap.

When your child or teen explains his opinions and feelings, give your attention with love and respect. You are reasoning together, so set the example of listening well.

Age Appropriateness

When communicating our expectations with our children, we need to make sure our requests are age-appropriate and within each child's ability. Each child is different, and we increase their chances of success when we are sensitive to their limitations.

A mother was frustrated because her young son never seemed to complete his chores without her constantly getting after him. She thought that he was rebellious and that her discipline needed to be tougher. One day, she took the time to give him one clear instruction at a time, and she noticed that he was completing each chore without the constant reminders. She realized that she had been giving him too many instructions at once. She decided from then on to boost his confidence by giving him one clear instruction at a time. As a result, their mutual frustrations were reduced.

Tips for Age Appropriateness

- Generally speaking, young children need one simple instruction at a time that calls for an immediate action.

- With older children or teens, you may be able to give them several instructions or expectations at once; the time frame to accomplish them can also be longer.

- Writing out your expectations is often helpful. You may want to use charts - or use your teen's technology against her. (Text or post to Facebook: "Remember to pick up your brother at school today at 3:30.") That'll get the job done.

Do you see how giving clear instructions and creating unambiguous expectations will reduce opportunities for arguments? Parents, it's up to us to set the tone for our leadership through our instructions. The clarity and focus of parents' communication is like a quarterback's clear signals to the team. His signal calling gives the team confidence in its leader and lets all the players know their role and understand what's expected of them.

A second trap that's closely related to the argument trap lurks in the next chapter. Parenting Trap #2 is Getting Played: Reasoning and Negotiating Everything.

Chapter 5

Parenting Tool #2: Standing Your Ground - Because You're the Parent

---

Parenting Trap #2
Getting Manipulated:
Reasoning and Negotiating Everything

Now we're ready to encounter the second parenting trap, Getting Manipulated: Reasoning and Negotiating Everything. We'll immediately follow with the second parenting tool, which will disarm the trap.

When parents see our Volcano illustration and look at the techniques on the left side that children use for arguing, they're usually surprised to see *reasoning* on the list. Then on the right side they again see *reasoning* listed as a parent's response to match their children's reasoning.

Must every family rule or requirement be reasonable? We say - absolutely not!

"Isn't reasoning a good thing?" After all, in Isaiah 1:18 the Lord invited us, "Come now, let us reason together." Absolutely - it's wonderful for a family to talk things over. However, the context of the Volcano illustration is that the parents have given instructions, and their children are avoiding or delaying getting them done.

What is this trap? It's when parents take the bait of justifying and negotiating everything. In this trap parents feel they need to answer to their children for all their standards, schedules, and family customs.

How effective is this trap in your home? Do you find the reasoning trap pulling you in like the monkey reaching for the coconut?

The Art of Negotiation:
Fun for Them, Not for You

Teachers have to work though this same minefield every day. In high school or college classes, apathetic students suddenly come alive when a quiz is announced or a test is looming. Out of the blue students have riveting questions about the material. Suddenly they're ready to tell you all about their lives and the fascinating events that impeded their studies, making today's test monumentally unfair and inappropriate. Didn't you just love negotiating everything on test day when you were a student? It was so much fun!

Teachers understand this trap and stand their ground. But parents often take the bait and find themselves justifying everything they do to their children.

As we discussed in chapters 3 and 4, reasoning can quickly become arguing, and then parents lose. The definition of *manipulate* includes, "To handle skillfully, to manage artfully or shrewdly, or in an unfair way."* Our children can have us wrapped around their finger from day one, skillfully handling us - Parenting Tool #2: Standing Your Ground.

Parenting Tool #2
Standing Your Ground

Must every family rule or requirement be reasonable? We say - absolutely not! You're the parent, and you're entitled to some eccentricities.

---

* *Webster's New World Dictionary* (Cleveland: Wiley Publishing, 2002)

One of the parents in our Parenting Partners leadership group told us that she felt like an unreasonable parent because of her children's early bedtimes. She talked about how guilty she felt for being so out of sync with the other parents in her neighborhood.

The details? Marcy is a single mother who feels totally spent after dinner. She's wasted. She needs some downtime. Therefore she puts her elementary age children to bed at 7:30, letting them read in bed until they fall asleep.

Marcy's family lives in a chaotic neighborhood where most families have no bedtimes for their children at all. The elementary-age kids typically stay up past midnight on school nights. So her children have asserted that she's "the worst mother in the world" for making them go to bed so early.

Our group loved this story and assured Marcy that she is the best mother on the block, not the worst. But it brought up the question, "Can a good parent be out of sync with other parents?" Do all the family rules need to accommodate everyone in the family, or can a parent use the old-fashioned standard, "Because I'm the parent"?

It's the Parent's Choice

You're not accountable to your children for every family routine or custom. Family meal at 5:30, 6 or 7 - it's your choice! Stand your ground.

Bath right after dinner. Bath every night. Shower instead of bath. Go crazy with power! You can make the rules! Stand your ground.

As parents, you have the right to make family routines and rules that work for your personality and needs. If you're a neat freak, by all means make rules for neatness that work for you. "At 8:00, everyone's things need to be out of the living room: toys, books, shoes, snakes, everything."

If you need a neat space to crash by 8:00, you're entitled - that's just how authoritative you are. Don't make the mistake of negotiating away your needs. Stand your ground.

You may hear, "Dad, we're the only family on earth who can't leave a shoe in the living room." "You're such a neat freak." Just remember that you're being baited; don't take the bait. Your rule doesn't need anyone's approval. Just embrace it:

- "Yes, I am the king of clean."
- "Yes, I'm eccentric that way."
- "I must be a pretty weird dad."

Owning your preferences takes the entertainment value out of fighting you.

Forget the Guilt

Don't feel a bit guilty! You make tremendous sacrifices for your children's healthy development. You accommodate their needs, wishes, and personalities constantly. Don't let them make you feel bad about insisting on room for your needs and personality.

Most children know how easy it is to make their parents feel guilty. It's like shooting ducks in a barrel! Marcy's children made her feel guilty for their 7:30 bedtimes. Some teens make their parents feel guilty for their curfew requirements, or parents' intrusions into their privacy, such as asking about their friends or "stalking" their social network postings.

We say, "Stand your ground." Parents are entitled to have family routines and policies that work for them. Don't get manipulated into feeling guilty.

We practice this principle ourselves. Most families enjoy vacations at the shore, on the beach. Our children had no such luck. When we take a trip, we want to be active. Why drive all the way to the ocean just to stop on the brink of the water to sit on the beach?

When our children were young, we bought a tandem ocean kayak. Now our children did not have the option of enjoying time on the beach. They had to hit the waves with their father. They sometimes liked this, but not always. They had to wonder, "Why can't we be normal sometimes and just sit around?"

On the positive side, our daughter was only five when she developed a talent for calling seals over to the boat, so we were seemingly always accompanied by a seal navy. When our son was eight, he and his dad traveled to Alaska and paddled to a remote inlet so far away that it taxed his patience. He was both pleased and relieved, however, when a guide said he was the youngest person to explore the inlet.

> **When we accept our uniqueness with humor, it both defuses arguments and shows that we care more about moral development than customs.**

Are those great memories for the children? Maybe, maybe not. But when we take time off, we do what works for us, and that doesn't involve leisure. Did we hear complaints? Oh yeah, but as parents we went crazy with power as we planned trips we liked. Other times we did what they liked best, like going to the Boardwalk. But we remembered to let some family travel and routines meet our needs as well.

The Challenges of Immigrant Families

A large percentage of families in our parent leadership workshops are recent immigrants to the United States or Canada. Because their children learn the new language and culture faster than parents, the young people have great power to play tricks on their parents.

We've listened to countless parents tell stories of how their children tried to pull the wool over their eyes, telling them how little power parents have in America. They commonly tell them how American law prohibits parents from disciplining their children. "In America, you can't make me do my homework," or "In America, you can't tell me what to do," are claims many of our parents hear.

These parents suspect the scam, but they're not entirely sure. Most are from traditional, family oriented cultures that place a premium on respecting elders and parents. They've heard that it's different in North America. As a result, many of them back away from their involvement in discipline, especially when their children enter middle school/ junior high school.

We love seeing the relief on these parents' faces when we tell them that they've been scammed, because they are in charge of their families in America as much as they were still in Mexico, Vietnam, India, Cuba, Columbia, or anywhere else. We usually include public leaders on our presenting teams, such as school principals, superintendents, pastors, doctors, and police officers, to reinforce this message. We include these leaders to assure parents that they are in charge after all, even in America, and that public servants are supporting the parents' authority and leadership.

> **Don't get sidetracked with arguments over family practices and routines. Don't take the bait.**

Isn't it great to know that parents can refuse to be manipulated away from positive discipline, and are free to guide their children's social and moral development?

Social Development

Parents are devoted to building both the social and moral capacity of their children. Parenting Tool #2 contributes to both. This "standing your ground" tool builds their social capacity in a number of ways:

1. Teaching them manners that are essentially universal.

Examples include:

- Put your towel on the towel rack.
- Hang up your clothes.
- Don't track mud in the house.

From toddlers to teenagers, we devote ourselves to civilizing our children by teaching them the discipline to have good manners and etiquette. We know that these social skills are critical for their future success.

How often do you think about "the future spouse standard"? You want your children to be sensitive and socially capable for their future marital partners. You don't want them to undergo the ordeal of hearing a spouse say, "Didn't your mother teach you _____ ?" Fill in the blank: to replace the toilet paper, to put away your dishes, to wash your clothes, to chew with your mouth closed. So we build their aptitude for meeting the social expectations of others.

2. Teaching them to pay attention to particular social protocol and customs.

Such as:

- Never use the guest towels.
- Don't wear your shoes in the house.
- Keep the cat outside.

Learning protocol enables your children to function in their culture and across cultures. Children learn some of this protocol within their extended families. One side of the family arrives early for every appointment, the other side fashionably late. Some families have formal meals; others have backyard barbeques.

This experience gives our children the flexibility they need to adapt to the idiosyncrasies of various families and cultures. This knowledge of protocol and cross-cultural customs opens doors for future success. It also helps them see the difference between customs and moral principles.

3. Modeling nondefensiveness around our distinctive customs.

Each parent and family has its own customs and idiosyncrasies. Our children often express their independence by becoming annoyed by these. They clash with our family customs and rules with "Why do we have to _____ ?"

We parents can contribute to the social and moral development of our children by not being defensive about our distinctive personal or family customs. When we accept our uniqueness with humor, it both defuses arguments and shows that we care more about moral development than customs. "Yes, I am the only father in town who makes you clean your room." "Yes, I am an extreme neat freak."

This allows you to distinguish family practices and customs that are a matter of your choice from the moral principles that are imperative for your child's moral development. When parents try to make every family rule into the will of God, it's bound to create a backlash of resentment later. There are only ten commandments, which are The Ten Commandments. Our rules for the family are great, but they're not moral principles, and we don't treat them with that level of gravity or dedication.

We can stand firm in expecting our children to do what we instruct and to respect our family rules and customs. We can also do that without taking the bait of arguing. This is so important that we're going to give you a tool to end the arguing in the next chapter - "the Shield."

4. Our ultimate goal is for our children's social development to graduate to moral development.

Social development elevates to moral development when "respect" appears. This is the attitude change from "I have to" to "I want to for your sake." We know that parents earnestly desire this moral formation, because we endlessly talk to our children about respect and attitude.

This step of moral development is encapsulated by Jesus' Golden Rule of "Do to others as you would have them do to you" (Luke 6:31). It is further expressed in the practical standard from Philippians 2:4, "Each of you should look not only to your own interests, but also to the interests of others."

Moral Development

What are moral principles? An example is the key developmental task of learning to be honest and to deal with temptations such as stealing and lying. We know that learning honesty is vital to a child's moral development and future success. As parents, we are willing to invest great time and effort into building their habits and hearts regarding honesty.

Here are some other examples of moral development:

- Standing up for the "least of these," such as advocating for a bullied student or a student new to the community (Matthew 25:40).
- Caring for one's health proactively and avoiding harmful substances.
- Being willing to deal with the consequences of an embarrassing grade rather than cheating to get a commendable grade.
- Learning to deal with illness and disappointment.
- Learning to love an enemy and do good to them (Luke 6:35).
- Growing in humility.

Robert Coles, the esteemed child psychiatrist who wrote extensively on the moral and spiritual life of children, discussed moral development by saying,

> *Good children are boys and girls who in the first place have learned to take seriously the very notion, the desirability, of goodness - a living up to the Golden Rule, a respect for others, a commitment of mind, heart, soul to one's family, neighborhood, nation - and have also learned that the issue of goodness is not an abstract one, but rather a concrete, expressive one: how to turn the rhetoric of goodness into action, moments that affirm the presence of goodness in a particular lived life.* *

As we devote time and energy to developing this sensibility in our children, we need to watch for opportunities. Teachable moments are valuable, especially when our children transgress. In addition to using such circumstances, we want to work creatively with our children on moral development. You can find practical resources for systematically building your children's moral and spiritual development at the Heritage Builders website: **www.heritagebuilders.com.**

What's our key principle? Don't get sidetracked with arguments over family practices and routines. Don't take the bait. Instead, save your focus and energy for investing in discipline that shapes the moral development of your children. Remember to stand your ground - because you're the parent!

---

*Robert Coles, *The Moral Intelligence of Children: How to Raise a Moral Child* (New York: Random House, 1997), p. 17.

Chapter 6

Parenting Tool #3: Deflecting Arguments with the Shield

Parenting Trap #3
Getting Trapped by Routine Conflicts

Parenting Trap #3 is Getting Trapped by Routine Conflicts. This trap will grind parents down, leaving them wondering, "Now why did I sign up to be a parent in the first place?" The trap then escalates into frustration, as illustrated by the volcano in Chapter 3.

As we saw in that chapter, children and teens often try to avoid or delay doing what parents ask them to do by reasoning or arguing the instruction, leading to conflicts with parents. Before we introduce the "deflecting arguments" tool, let's review how routine conflicts develop.

Examples of Routine Conflicts

Do you notice that most arguments are over daily routines? That it's the same argument every day or every week?

If you don't want to get drawn into an argument with your children, you need a shield that sets a boundary and deflects the argument.

You may have noticed that these arguments usually occur right when parents get home or in the evening. Why? Because parents are tired, and children are wound up. Children know how to time arguments to give themselves the advantage.

Here are some examples of common parent/child conflicts:

- Watching TV before doing homework.
- Not eating breakfast.
- Curfews.
- Using the car.
- Dinner with family vs. going to a friend's house.
- Home dinner vs. fast food.
- Turning off video games and TV.
- Going to bed on time.
- Brushing teeth or taking baths.

What are some of the routine conflicts that your children create?

So you recognize the routine conflicts trap. Now what can you do about it?

Introducing the Shield

This trap has met its match in the third parenting tool, the Shield. It looks simple - but it's powerful! If you have time to master just one parenting tool, this is the one!

Take a look at "The Shield" illustration titled "Deflect: Don't Argue." What does a shield do?

The person holding the Shield is protected from battle, doesn't get drawn into a fight, and deflects the attack.

If you don't want to get drawn into an argument with your children, you need a shield that sets a boundary and deflects the argument.

Look at the illustration titled "Deflect, Don't Argue." As you can see, the shield prevents us from being manipulated; it keeps us from being trapped into an argument.

The Shield in this illustration contains two words. These two words alone more than repay the price of this book:

- *Nevertheless*
- *Regardless*

These words act like a shield for routine arguments. We're offering these two words, but you only need one of them, since they're synonymous. So pick a word, and check out this example.

Here's How it Works

The Shield is a simple three-step process:

1. **You give your child a direction.**

   For example, "Matt, it's time to go to bed now."

2. **Your child begins to argue.**

   "But I went to bed early last night," or "My TV show is almost over."

3. **You respond with a Shield direction.**

   "Nevertheless, I need you to go to bed now."

Whatever the child says, you simply respond with either "nevertheless" or "regardless" and then repeat your instruction firmly but calmly.

- For example, he may say, "But I have all my homework done, and it won't take me long to get ready for bed."
- Your response will still be "Nevertheless, I need you to go to bed now."

Here's the most important tip: Do not add anything to your instruction.

- Just say "nevertheless" or "regardless," and then simply repeat your initial instruction like a broken record.

- The minute you add anything to your instructions, you open yourself up for a long conversation and a power struggle, as we saw in the section with the volcano!

Using the Shield will lead you to give simple instructions. You may have to repeat them several times, so choose simple instructions from the start.

Also, the Shield will help you deliver instructions without the "why." **An instruction with reasons invites discussion. A brief instruction invites action.**

Practicing with the Shield

When we present the Shield in our parenting groups, we always take the time to let everyone practice. Why? Because this tool doesn't feel natural. Our normal inclination when giving our children instructions is to explain, explain, explain. Explain some more, then discuss, then debate. This tool is completely different - it's simple and basic. It could feel a little weird.

So if you can, practice this with another adult before you unleash it on your children.

It is a simple strategy, but extremely effective. When your children see that you are committed to being in control and that you will not be drawn into an argument, they will realize there is no use arguing. They will do what is expected.

Give it a try! As we've taught this to thousands of parents, the first reaction is often "You don't know my kid." Regardless, the next week they return with success stories.

Look again at the "Deflect: Don't Argue" illustration. Use "Nevertheless" or "Regardless" as your Shield to deflect arguments.

As you practice, remember to:
- **Stand strong.**
- **Use few words.**

- **Be firm.**
- **Don't engage.**
- **Repeat like a broken record.**

When you practice using the Shield, take turns playing the part of the child and the part of the parent. Pick one of the examples from our list of routine conflicts, or you can use an example from your own experience at home.

This probably feels different from what you usually do when your children start arguing with you. Do you think your children might cooperate if you stand your ground?

Did you notice as you practiced using the Shield that there is a lack of drama? The parent using the Shield is very calm and unexciting. This takes all the fun out of arguing!

With younger children, you can use "even so" as easier words instead of "nevertheless." On the other hand, "nevertheless" works well even with the younger ones because it's a strange word that gets their attention

GIT-R-DONE!!!

The Shield is a specialty tool, designed for a specific job. The job is getting your children to do what you instruct.

The purpose of this parenting tool is to GIT-R-DONE!! (Thank you, Larry the Cable Guy.)

The Shield is a practical life skill. When we ask parents for stories of how they used the Shield with their children, they often say, "I've been using it with adults more. At the hotel front desk, 'Nevertheless, I have a reservation.' At work, 'Regardless, I need to go home now.' It's just a non-argumentative way of presenting our needs and asserting our boundaries.

Because the Shield is a reasonable approach to standing up for ourselves with other adults, it's an appropriate approach to our teens. "Nevertheless, I need you to fill the car with gas after you use it" may not be music to your son's ears, but it's a positive alternative to an argument or to expressing frustration.

Secret Weapon: the Power of Boredom

Boredom is the kryptonite to your child's superpowers. It neutralizes their energy and ability to avoid work you've assigned. When you use the Shield, please be as boring as possible. That may take some acting from someone as naturally interesting as you, but give it a try.

Any drama from the parent will create the delay and entertainment that your child is angling for (remember the Five Reasons Kids Argue). Who would have thought that parents have this secret weapon? We do have the power, after all.

> **Boredom is the kryptonite to your child's superpowers.**

When you use the Shield, you don't need to be intense. You don't need "the look." You can be absolutely calm. You can be tired - the Shield saves your energy. Remember the power of boredom.

The Shield is a Real Game Changer

Do you remember the story we told in Chapter 3 of the preschooler who created an argument with her mother every day? The little girl argued for dinner at McDonald's or Taco Bell. The mother felt frustrated that she took the bait day after day and always felt manipulated. She felt annoyed and angry. She knew her daughter was pushing her buttons but didn't know what to do about it. When we showed her the Shield technique, she felt her daughter was so strong-willed that she would fight it.

This mother applied the Shield, and it worked perfectly. She became much more confident and settled in her parenting ability. She said, "So this is what it feels like to be the parent!"

We call that feeling "the Parent Zone." It's the feeling that you have authority. Just as teachers, police officers, or managers have authority because of their jobs, you as a parent have authority - just because you're the parent. Now this mom experienced that: her authority is from her calling as a parent, not from being able to convince her children. That's "the Parent Zone."

About a year after this mother starting using the Shield, David spoke in her church and met the family. When the daughter, Amy, heard that he had taught her mother about the Shield, she said, "My mother and I don't argue anymore. Now we have lots of extra time. We use our time to walk around the mall, and we paint each other's toes."

The mother also added the story that one time Amy's younger brother started arguing with his mother. He's normally very cooperative, so she was surprised. Then she heard Amy calling out from the next room, "Mom, say 'nevertheless.'" The whole family cracked up.

How Long do you Persist, and What if it Doesn't Work?

Our parents sometimes ask, how many times do you repeat your Shield instructions?

Our experience is that about 80 percent of the time children or young people will stop arguing and cooperate after, at the most, three repetitions of "Nevertheless, time for bed."

About 10 percent of the time children are more creative with their arguments and persist for more than four repetitions. But after they test it out a few times, they realize it's a waste of their energy (and it's boring) and thereafter stop arguing when they hear "nevertheless."

After parents establish this tool in their household, children will usually comply as soon as a parent says "nevertheless" or "regardless." In a few instances children become defiant when they hear the key word. In those cases, we move directly to Parenting Tool #5, Applying Consequences, in the next chapter.

Don't Take the Bait

After mastering the Shield, parents realize that they don't have to take the bait and that they don't have to get into arguments with their children. With the Shield, we're protected from the parent traps our children set to avoid our instructions and evade discipline. Now parents are in the zone, and our kids and teens benefit from positive discipline.

Many parents in Parenting Partners workshops report that the Shield is their favorite! It's a powerful tool that gives parents the confidence that they can give instructions while standing firm and staying in control.

Chapter 7

Parenting Tool #4:
Confidence in the
Value of Positive Discipline

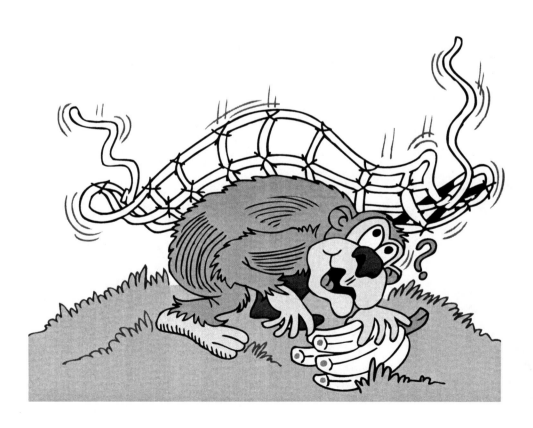

Manageable Discipline

When parents start applying the first three parenting tools, they find that discipline in their home improves so much that there are now fewer instances when consequences need to be administered. Before parents begin using these tools, there is so much conflict that they are forever threatening consequences that are difficult to apply consistently. With these tools, however, family life is more manageable, and parents are actually able to implement a more positive and consistent system of discipline.

We'll use the next three chapters and three parenting tools for the subject of positive discipline and consequences. In this chapter we work with Parenting Trap #4: Confusing Discipline and Punishment. We'll then disentangle parents from that trap with Parenting Tool #4: Confidence in the Value of Discipline.

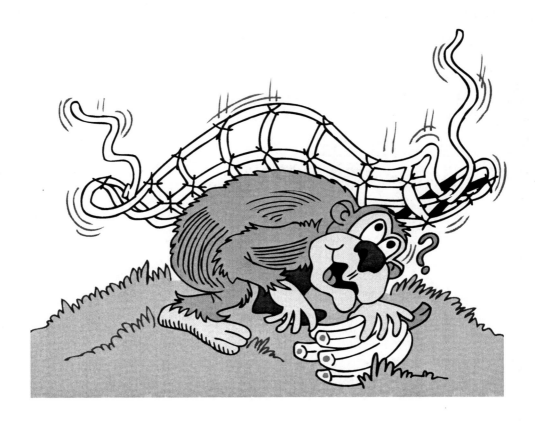

Parent Trap #4
Confusing Discipline and Punishment

Sometimes our children need a little extra help to motivate them to follow instructions. What do you do when your children misbehave? Do you bring on the discipline by using consequences, dish out punishment, or let them get away with it?

Our experience is that parents often think of administering discipline as "punishing" their children. That usually creates some mixed feelings. When parents feel that discipline is less than positive, they can start feeling guilty about imposing discipline.

How do we discover the difference between discipline and punishment and find guilt-free discipline? To reinforce our confidence in the value of discipline and consequences, let's nail down the difference between discipline and punishment.

Definition of Discipline

What is the difference between discipline and punishment? Please take a look at our illustration with that same name.

We define discipline as:

- Training or learning that develops strong character, self-control, and moral capacity.
- Training that empowers a person to learn from mistakes and be equipped for success next time.

Which part of this definition do you find most valuable?

In Chapter 2, we first developed the value of discipline on the foundation of Hebrews 12. Discipline is indispensable for our children's future success, relationships, and spiritual formation! It's one of the greatest gifts a parent can give.

In Chapter 1, we also explained that discipline becomes the skill set that empowers your children to fulfill their potential. It equips them to develop a growing spiritual life, to create healthy relationships, and to succeed in school and vocation. It becomes the ultimate gift from parents to children.

> While punishment says, "I give up on you," discipline says, "I believe in you." It's a spectacular contrast.

Definition of Punishment

Compare the definition of punishment:

- Imposing a penalty for breaking a rule or the law, often in retaliation.
- Dealing with roughly or harshly; castigating.

How does this explanation of punishment contrast with that of discipline?

Our Parenting Partners book is in Spanish as well as English. The Spanish terms highlight the contrast between these two approaches:

- Discipline is Disciplina.
- Punishment is Castigo.

Discipline vs. Castigation. Would you rather be disciplined or castigated when you make a mistake? Which would you want to encounter at work if you messed up a project?

- Disciplina, which is to learn from your mistakes and be equipped for success next time? or
- Castigo, which is an attack on you as a person: "How could you be so stupid, so defective, so incapable, so worthless?"

Relating to Discipline and Punishment

It's easy for us to relate to discipline and punishment. We want people to build us up with discipline, not to tear us down with castigation. We want the adults who teach, mentor, and coach our sons and daughters to do the same for them.

Does the definition of punishment remind you of the erupting volcano? When the volcano is erupting, are we more likely to respond with discipline or punishment? It reminds you that parents usually use punishment when they're feeling emotional, especially when they're feeling discouraged. Punishment says, "I don't know what to do with you." It expresses hopelessness or resignation.

> **Positive discipline equips our children to be resilient in the face of hardship.**

While punishment says, "I give up on you," discipline says, "I believe in you." It's a spectacular contrast. Punishment has lost heart with discouragement; discipline is always hopeful. It expresses faith that your child or teen can learn and grow. Giving discipline is giving love, and love "always protects, always trusts, always hopes, always perseveres" (1 Corinthians 13:7).

By the way, we find that many parents use the word *punishment* as shorthand when they mean "consequences." We encourage parents to adopt the words *discipline or consequences* when they mean "consequences."

Discipline:	Punishment:

- Training or learning that develops strong character, self-control, and moral capacity.

- Training that empowers a person to learn from mistakes and be equipped for success next time.

- Imposing a penalty for breaking a rule or the law; often in retaliation.

- Dealing with roughly or harshly; castigating.

The Six Characteristics of Discipline

1. Provides direction and correction.
2. Values learning from mistakes.
3. Focuses on the future.
4. Attitude of love and support.
5. Directed at the behavior.
6. Promotes security and self-control.

The Six Characteristics of Punishment

1. Inflicts a penalty.
2. Requires perfection.
3. Focuses on the past.
4. Attitude of anger and retaliation.
5. Directed at the individual.
6. Promotes fear, resentment and anxiety.

Child learns:

- responsibility
- self-control
- to be a learner
- to recover from mistakes
- to see self as a winner
- to see self as okay
- positive self-identity

Child learns:

- not to get caught
- to avoid punishment
- to lie and be sneaky
- to manipulate the system
- to see self as a failure
- to see self as not okay
- negative self-identity

Six Characteristics of Discipline

In the illustration "The Difference between Discipline and Punishment," what are the characteristics of discipline that are superior to the characteristics of punishment?

1. Discipline provides direction and correction.

Parents have to summon the energy to confront and correct their children when they fall into bad habits or make mistakes. As parents increasingly believe in the positive power of discipline, they'll invest more time and energy into discipline.

2. Discipline values learning from mistakes.

How do you feel when your children make mistakes? Do you worry about the inconvenience involved in correcting those mistakes and fixing the messes, or are you excited about the learning opportunities that have popped up? Thomas Edison is famous for his attitude toward the thousands of mistakes he made during his process of inventing the light bulb. He said, **"Results! Why, man, I have gotten a lot of results. I know several thousand things that won't work."**

Do children and young people need to make mistakes in order to create opportunities for their moral, mental, and social development? We believe they do. Parents then go to work utilizing the raw material of mistakes to teach. Parents love to teach, right? So can parents approach children with love and enthusiasm when they set the stage for these learning experiences?

Will children look forward to these learning opportunities? Hardly—it feels like punishment to them. But parents know that each learning opportunity is a step forward for our child's development.

3. Discipline focuses on the future.

When parents discipline their children, they are expressing confidence in their potential. Discipline is based on hope, so it builds for the future. It creates a pathway to change.

4. Discipline is done in an attitude of love and support.

Discipline is focused on giving to our children. We're giving them knowledge and skills for their future well-being, so we can discipline with confidence. How difficult is this for parents during times when we're rushed or exhausted?

Disciplining and guiding our children takes a tremendous investment of our time. Can you imagine how many hours each parent invests in discipline and teaching each child on an annual basis? It's a huge commitment. But have your financial investments ever paid off like these investments?

Have you tried thinking of those hours as being like money you are investing in your children's college fund? It takes sacrifice, but it shows how much you believe in them.

5. Discipline is directed at the behavior.

In our workshops, this is the contrast that parents talk about most often. They suddenly realize how they typically start with instructions, and then when the child doesn't comply, they move to "what's wrong with you?"

We can relate to this ourselves, in terms of our workplace. I can let down my guard when a co-worker tells me how he wants a job done in a particular way. I can learn to do it differently next time. It's not personal - I'm just meeting his needs and specifications.

6. Discipline promotes a sense of security and self-control.

Like the illustration of the Den of Belonging in chapter 2, discipline helps our children feel confident and secure. Positive discipline equips them to be resilient in the face of hardship, as the Hebrews 12:7-11 passage revealed.

Six Characteristics
of Punishment

1. Punishment inflicts a penalty.

Discipline restores relationships and creates a glimpse of God's Shalom relationship with us. Punishment separates parents and children. The feeling is "get away from me" rather than "let's get together."

Most judicial systems punish people for breaking the law rather than restoring violated relationships. Law breakers are fined or put away in prison. How well does prison work to prevent future law breaking?

2. Punishment requires perfection.

Punishment, by contrast, does not allow for growth. It assumes that the child must be perfect, and every mistake is a step backwards. How can children win in this system? They can't. It's discouraging and hopeless. Their only options are to mask their mistakes with cover-ups or to give up and rebel.

3. Punishment focuses on the past.

Punishment clings to the past: "You always …" "You never …" Punishment keeps a record of past mistakes and brings them up repeatedly, overwhelming and discouraging the child. "I can't do anything right." "I'll never be good enough."

By contrast, discipline focuses on the future and communicates hopefulness, grace, and the pathway to change. Again, giving discipline is giving love, and love "is not easily angered, it keeps no record of wrongs" (1 Corinthians 13:5).

4. Punishment is administered with an attitude of anger and retaliation.

In our parent leadership workshops we have graduation programs in which parents talk about which skills have improved their parenting the most.

Increasingly, many parents have reported that learning the difference between punishment and discipline was vital for them.

They report that when they were raised in family systems that replied on punishment in anger, so they came to accept that as a show of love. They came to feel that was the kind of love they deserved. Now they understand that the love demonstrated in discipline is far superior.

5. Punishment is directed at the person.

In the "Discipline is directed at the behavior" section above, we discussed how we trust co-workers who tell us how they want us to do a task differently in order to meet their specifications.

However, if the co-worker's critique becomes personal, the focus is no longer on the task; it's now on the co-worker and me. I now must focus my energy on managing a difficult person who is castigating me. I may be inclined to defend or protect myself.

Likewise, if we want our child to learn something or get something done, we must focus only on the job and not let it spill over into a personal critique.

6. Punishment promotes fear, resentment, and anxiety.

Because a punishment-based family system requires perfection, children then feel like they have to walk on eggshells. Their energy is directly toward not getting caught, or learning not to care about the consequences when they are caught.

What Children Learn from Punishment

Children learn far different lessons from punishment than from discipline. Look at the bottom right section of the illustration "The Difference between Discipline and Punishment." Here we see what children learn from punishment:

- Punishment teaches a child not to get caught, to avoid punishment, to lie and to be sneaky and to manipulate the system.
- Punishment causes our children to see themselves as failures and to believe that they are not "okay."
- Punishment promotes negative self-identity and low self-esteem.

Punishment is like starting a game of bowling with 300 points. Then each time we fail to get a strike points are deducted. It's a game of demerits. It always feels like a game of survival, and children function like they are trying to survive: manipulating, dodging detection, picking every word carefully.

Punishment can Feel Dismissive

Discipline requires an investment of time. Punishment does not, so it can feel dismissive. In punishment, parents sometimes make comments that sound like they don't care:

- "Whatever."
- "Forget it."
- "Do whatever you want."
- "I give up."

Children can feel that these comments mean that the parent is walking away from them. Giving up on them. Each of these comments is a dagger to our children's hearts - an attack on the person, not the behavior. Even as adults, we take dismissive comments personally because they feel so destructive.

> **Discipline requires an investment of time. Punishment does not, so it can feel dismissive.**

What Children Learn from Discipline

Look at the bottom left section of the illustration "The Difference between Discipline and Punishment." Here we see what children learn from discipline:

- Discipline teaches our children responsibility and self-control.
- Discipline helps our children to be learners and to grow from their mistakes. This is resiliency.
- Discipline encourages our children to see themselves as winners and to believe they are "okay."
- Discipline helps our children develop a positive self-identity.

Resiliency

We could write a chapter on any one of these benefits children gain from discipline. Our favorite may be resiliency. If there is one strength or proficiency that gives parents peace of mind, it's that our children know how to recover from hardships and mistakes. They know how to make lemonade when life gives them lemons.

What a great inheritance that is! If you leave your children money, they'll probably spend it and be no further ahead. But if you give them resiliency, they can handle economic downturns, office politics, illness, and all kinds of disappointment. Most important, they can handle disappointment as an affirmation of God's love toward them. (See the section in Chapter 2 on Hebrews 12.)

Is Discipline Easy?

What time do you get up in the morning to take care of your kids or get to work? Certainly that isn't easy. How many hours do you work at your job and at home? Your schedule is an example of how you live a disciplined life.

Should we expect less of our children?

How much of a parent's effort is required for discipline? Discipline requires a substantial investment from any parent. It requires time, thought, and effort.

Situations of discipline and consequences are teachable moments. Not all our parenting skills involve teachable moments. The Shield in Chapter 6 is not a teachable moment because the child or teen already knows what to do. However, the situations in this chapter open up teachable moments.

Discipline is Practice for Success

Sports Practice → **Great Game!**

Music Practice → **Great Performance!**

Good Study Habits → **Academic Success!**

Discipline is
Practice for Success

Does discipline reminds you of training for sports or music? Look at our illustration "Discipline is Practice for Success."

When our children are on sports teams, how do they feel about going to practices? Practice can be unpleasant, with repetitive drills and boring laps. Yet is the coach out to get them, or is he building their skills to succeed in the game?

Training isn't fun like the actual game, but without training the game itself wouldn't be much fun either.

And who likes music practice when first learning to play an instrument? Yet when you attend the performance, you are happy that your child had the discipline to practice, aren't you?

Discipline Builds
Positive Identity

Discipline is a powerful factor in building the self-esteem and positive identity of young people. How does discipline build the positive identity of a teen or child? It shows our son or daughter:

"I am loved!"
- If we don't bother with discipline, young people don't feel included and valuable.

- When we do invest in discipline, they know we support them and love them.

"I am capable!"

- When we invest in discipline, young people know that we have high expectations for them and that we trust them.
- When we invest in discipline, young people know we believe in them and their future.
- When we invest in discipline, young people learn that they can recover and move on from their mistakes.

"I belong."

- When we invest in discipline, young people feel that they belong in the family.
- How would a child feel if you adopted her into your family, but treated her differently from your other children? How would she feel if she did not have the same responsibilities or expectations that the other children had?

The Example of Restorative Justice: The Power of Positive Discipline

An example of the power of positive discipline is found in the practice of "Family Conferencing" or "Restorative Justice" as an alternative to the traditional criminal justice system in dealing with young first-time offenders. This is a practice that communities around the world are implementing to reduce crime and cut government costs. It typically receives strong support from law enforcement leaders.

In the traditional criminal justice system, young people who commit a property crime often receive light, if any, penalties for their actions. They often learn to disrespect the system.

What percentage of juvenile offenders then commits another crime? Studies show up to 95 percent.

In a system of Restorative Justice, juvenile offenders do a Family Conference rather than go through the court system. In Family Conferencing, the young person meets with a mediator and:

- His or her parents, grandparents, aunts and uncles,
- The citizen victimized by the crime, and
- His or her teachers, youth leaders, religious leaders.

What do they do in that conference?

- The young person takes responsibility for his or her actions and crime and proposes a plan of restitution.
- The young person reconciles with the citizen victimized by the crime.
- The family and community members take roles in creating more structure and accountability for the young person: Grandpa will pick you up from school on Monday, Aunt Marie on Tuesday, etc.

Now, how many of these young people commit another crime? According to studies, only five percent re-offend.

These young people never want to do another Family Conference. This is a discipline that's painful! They learn respect and responsibility. They receive support and structure from their family and community.

Law enforcement leaders around the world support it because this discipline is twenty times more successful than punishment strategies. Not only does it give young people a better future, but it saves the government millions of dollars by turning youth into productive citizens and preventing crime.

When we invest in discipline, young people know we believe in them and their future.

If positive discipline makes sense for the community, it certainly is the way to go at home! In the next chapter we'll find practical strategies for implementing positive discipline. Get ready for Parenting Tool #5.

Chapter 8

Parenting Tool #5:
Applying
Consequences

Parenting Trap #5
Avoiding Setting Consequences

Prior to picking up tools like the Shield, parents' time and energy were consumed with arguments and matching wits with their children. There wasn't much left for investing in applying consequences. Parents' get-up-and-go had got-up-and-went. The result: parents avoided giving consequences, and children missed out on learning from their mistakes.

> **Because we parents are calm and in control, we can have fun with consequences.**

Now, with Parenting Tools #1 - 4, all that has changed. Tools like the Shield take the drama and emotional payoff out of children's efforts to divert parents from discipline.

With Parenting Tool #5, parents can bring on the creativity, fun, and drama. Consequences are learning tools, and parents love to teach. Because we parents are calm and in control, we can have fun with consequences.

Consequences are the Weight Room of Moral Development

What are consequences?

- They are training tools that give children the mental and moral capacity to develop positive actions and habits.

- In short, consequences are the weight room that builds the strength to act morally and to successfully get along with others.

What is the role of a parent in administering consequences?

- The parent is a personal trainer for children, teaching them workout skills (moral and interpersonal actions and habits) and supporting them in their workout routines.

- A parent, like a personal trainer, teaches skills, provides motivation to build the right habits, and ensures safety during training.

In I Corinthians 9:25, Paul compares spiritual discipline to sports training.

Everyone who competes in the games goes into strict training. They do it to get a crown that will not last; but we do it to get a crown that will last forever.

Paul ministered in the Greek culture, which loved the Olympic Games. They knew that a young athlete's coach provides training out of love and commitment. Isn't that also the role of parents? We're coaches and personal trainers, hitting the weight room and running laps with our children.

As we build our children's moral capacity, we practice what we preach with integrity. We don't drive around in a golf cart as they run laps; we're running alongside them. We subject ourselves to the same discipline and live with the same consequences. We're totally committed to our children's growth.

Consequences Build Both Moral and Social Capacity

As we discussed in Chapter 5, moral capacity involves growth in integrity, responsibility, kindness, humility, self-control, and loving our neighbors. You can think of the Fruit of the Spirit, the Ten Commandments, and the Sermon on the Mount as content for moral development. Certainly the entirety of Jesus' ministry and teaching provide the content for our moral development.

Social capacity is simply our skill in getting along with people. These skills are not necessarily moral absolutes. One teacher wants the classroom calm and tidy; the next teacher wants it loud and creative. One parent wants the dishes washed right after the meal; another parent wants the family to linger in conversation. One family wants guests to make their beds; the next wants them left unmade.

Just like a trainer motivates an athlete, consequences motivate our children to build good habits.

Learning these expectations is important to future success in employment, school, and relationships. However, they're more confusing for children to learn, since they're based on the personal preferences of various people rather than on absolutes.

When we administer consequences, certainly we want to put the most energy into building moral capacity. It can be easier to put more energy into building social capacity, especially correcting the habits that personally annoy us, so we have to take care to focus on moral development.

Why do we Need Consequences?

What would you say consequences accomplish? When we ask parents in our workshops that question, they list, for example:

- They are extremely effective for changing children's behavior.
- They eliminate power struggles, arguing, and complaining.
- They develop responsibility in children while building self-esteem.

Parents also mention the power of consequences to motivate. Just like a trainer motivates an athlete, consequences motivate us to build good habits. No one, adult or child, will readily do things they don't want to do.

- Who would choose to do the dishes if they could just put their feet up and watch television?
- Who would go to work if they could just take vacation all the time and not worry about paying the bills?

Consequences are a necessary and natural part of life. When we give children consequences, we teach them responsibility and prepare them for the real world.

Two Types of Consequences

Look at the illustration, "Two Types of Consequences." These two types are called natural and logical. As you can see:

- **Natural consequences** happen without any intervention on our part.

  For natural consequences to work, we need to stay out of the way and let nature take its course.

- **Logical consequences** have to be generated by an authority figure, in this case a parent.

For logical consequences to work, parents set up the teaching environment by choosing a consequence for a situation and then taking action by administering that consequence.

Can you think of examples of natural consequences?

- Don't turn in your homework - you get a bad grade.
- Don't show up for work - you get fired.
- Don't change your car's oil - the car breaks down.

Can you think of examples of logical consequences?

- A child leaves his basketball outside - the parent takes it away for two days.
- A child watches TV instead of doing homework - she loses TV privileges this week.
- A teenager skips class - he is not allowed to use the car over the weekend.

Which consequences are better: natural or logical? Trick question - they're both vital. As you decide when to use natural consequences and when to use logical ones, you'll think about how your children learn and their personalities. If they continually leave their skateboards outside, how will they best learn to break that habit: if parents put the skateboards in time-out for a week, or if the skateboards are stolen or broken? We'll give you some examples now.

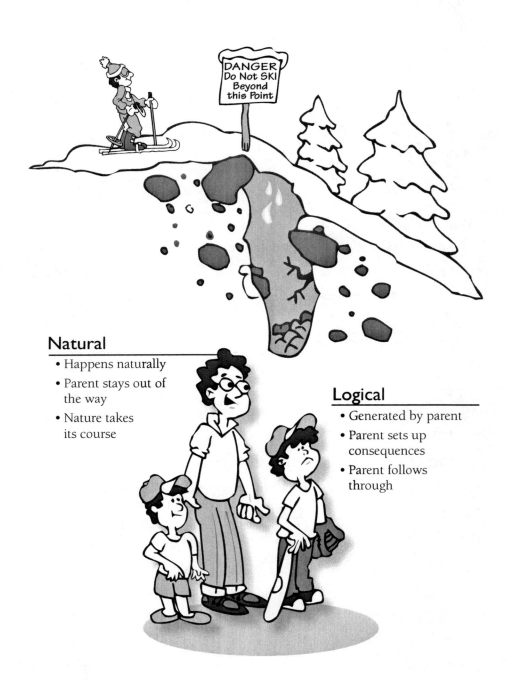

DANGER Do Not SKI Beyond this Point

Natural

- Happens naturally
- Parent stays out of the way
- Nature takes its course

Logical

- Generated by parent
- Parent sets up consequences
- Parent follows through

Practice Using
Natural Consequences

The best way to master the two kinds of consequences is with real-life examples. We will start by practicing natural consequences. To review:

- Natural consequences result from a child experiencing the reality of nature, requiring no action or intervention from the parent.
- In other words, if the parent stays out of the way, nature will take its course, and the consequence will do its work.

How would you apply natural consequences to these situations?

Problem 1: School Lunch

A ten-year-old forgets to take his lunch to school several times a week. By now, he is used to Mom bringing it to him at school.

What should you do in this situation?

Natural consequence: The parent does not deliver his lunch. The child does not like the choices in the school cafeteria and gets hungry.

Problem 2: Teen Money Choices

A dad gives his teenage daughter money to purchase some clothes. She then spends the money on movies and lunch, but she still wants to buy a pair of jeans at her favorite store. She pleads with her parents to pay for the jeans "just this once," even though this has happened several times before.

What should you do in this situation?

Natural consequence: The parents stay out of the way, i.e., they don't rescue their daughter from her mistakes. She made the choice to spend her clothes money on movies. The natural consequence is that she cannot buy the jeans.

Practice Using Logical Consequences

Now, let's get some practice using logical consequences. To review:

- Logical consequences are when an adult intervenes using a consequence that is logically related to the misbehavior.
- You might say that the goal is to custom-design the consequence to fit the behavior or habit you want to change.

How would you apply logical consequences to these situations?

Problem 1: Coloring on Walls

A five-year-old loves to color, particularly on the walls. She believes her artwork is beautiful but needs to learn that coloring is appreciated on paper, not on walls. Although she has been repeatedly directed to color on paper instead, she continues to draw on the wall.

What should you do in this situation?

Logical consequence: The child must clean the marks off the wall before she can have her crayons back.

Can you see how the consequence is directly related to the behavior in this example? It is important for the child to see the cause-and-effect relationship between the consequence and the behavior that brought it on.

Can you see how the consequence will be an effective teacher in this situation?

Remember that discipline is about teaching our children to recognize through experience what they need to do differently in the future. This is where logical consequences are extremely helpful.

Problem 2: Toys All Over the House

The parents are constantly tripping over their son's and daughter's Legos®. The children have been told to pick up their toys when they are done playing.

However, they always leave their toys all over the house, and the parents are tired of picking up after them.

What should you do in this situation?

Logical consequence: If the children do not put away the toys, the parent picks them up and keeps them in a special place. The parent does not allow the children to play with the toys for a few days and then perhaps has them do extra chores to buy them back.

More Practice Applying Logical Consequences

How would you apply logical consequences to the following situations?

Problem 1: Cleaning the Room

The household rule is that the children's bedrooms must be clean before their friends can come over. Joey wants to have a friend come over after school on Monday, but he did not clean his room, even though he was reminded of the rule.

What should you do in this situation?

Logical consequence: No friends over that day. Or he must clean his room before friends can come over.

Problem 2: Getting Up for School

Rachel has a persistent problem getting up for school on time.

What should you do in this situation?

Logical consequence: Rachel goes to bed one hour earlier. This may mean missing a favorite television show.

Problem 3: On Time for Dinner

Dinner is served at 6:00 p.m. Your teenager arrives home at 7:15 p.m. after staying at the park to play basketball with friends.

What should you do in this situation?

Logical consequence: He is grounded from the park for a few days.

You may have different ideas about which consequence is best, depending on what behavior you are trying to shape: being home on time for dinner, calling if staying out later than planned, or resisting the influence of friends.

Problem 4: Homework First

The family rule is no TV until homework is finished. The child consistently tells his parents he has finished his homework, even though he hasn't, so that he can watch TV.

What should you do in this situation?

Logical consequence: No TV at all during the school week, or grounded from TV for the following day each time the problem is discovered. Parents monitor his homework assignment log.

Eight Guidelines for Logical Consequences

Logical consequences are a powerful teaching tool. In order to create the greatest benefit, we suggest that you devise logical consequences around these eight guidelines.

Look at the illustration "Eight guidelines to remember when setting logical consequences."

Consequences must:

1. Be put into action without anger.

- If you are angry, you will not be able to use logical consequences effectively.

- Remember our volcano. If we are erupting, we are definitely not thinking clearly!

Consequences must:

1. Be put into action without anger.

2. Be communicated first.

3. Be perceived by the child as negative.

4. Relate to the misbehavior.

5. Allow freedom of choice.

6. Be age-appropriate and reasonable.

7. Be allowed to work.

8. Be manageable for the parents.

Sorry Tommy, we're going to McBurgers for lunch, but you haven't finished mowing the lawn. Guess you will have to miss-out!

2. Be communicated first.

- It is important to communicate with children first. Tell them the consequence - that is, what will happen if they continue the undesired behavior.

- Children need to hear from you that a consequence will be applied. This gives them the choice to control their behavior.

3. Be perceived by the child as negative.

- The consequence must be unpleasant in order for it to be effective.

- For example, if you send your child to his room, but the room is one of his favorite places to be because it has a television, video games, and internet, this will not be an effective consequence!

4. Relate to the misbehavior.

- The consequence should be logically related to the misbehavior.

- If your children color on the wall and the consequence is they can't watch TV, this is not related to the misbehavior. Scrubbing the wall would be a related and more effective consequence.

5. Allow freedom of choice.

- Children should have the freedom to make their own choices, to choose to change the behavior or accept the consequence. Children are resilient. It is important that they learn from their mistakes as well as their successes.

- If we do not allow our children to make the wrong choices, they will not have the opportunity to learn that other choices may be better!

6. Be age-appropriate and reasonable.

- Be sure that the task is within the child's capabilities and that it is reasonable.

- It is also important to keep consequences reasonable and age-appropriate.

- For example, it is not reasonable to ground a child for three months for arriving home late for dinner one night, nor is it reasonable to expect a young child to pull weeds for three hours.

7. Be allowed to work.

- Stay out of the way, and let the consequence do the correcting.
- This step is where many parents have a problem. We often threaten to take action with a consequence, but we're not prepared to follow through on that action.

8. Be manageable for the parents.

- The consequence can only work if you can monitor it. Think about what is practical for you.
- For example, if your child is having a temper tantrum in the grocery store and you threaten to leave the store if the tantrum does not stop, you should be prepared to follow through and leave the store.
- You must believe that giving the consequence is worth the inconvenience it causes you. Do not promise a consequence you are not able to carry out.

The Truth about Consequences - They can be Creative!

The Shield removed the entertainment value from arguing with a parent. It was a drama drain. It was boring.

However, the parent can be creative and dramatic with logical consequences that fit the eight guidelines. Our middle-school parents seem to be especially creative. Here are some real-life examples:

Rita's newly minted teenager was starting to experiment with marijuana and was storing his stash in his room. She knew that he valued his privacy above all.

- Among the consequences for drug use: she removed his door and put it into storage for two weeks.

- This door time-out made a great impression on him. Consequences are for teaching, and he decided privacy was more important than impressing his friends with drug use.

Parents have told us many stories of consequences that landed the bedroom door in timeout. For instance, it's often been a consequence for slamming the door in anger.

Tony's eighth-grader started skipping classes at school. Tony announced that the consequence for future skipping would be Dad attending the classes for him and sitting at his desk. He let his son know that the teachers had agreed to phone Dad if his son missed classes.

- Tony's son found the motivation to make it to every class.
- We've talked with many parents who have announced this consequence to their teenagers. Only a few have needed to enforce it, and then only once.

Logical consequences can be theatrical! You're not angry; you're just teaching. Therefore your teaching methods can be staged in a memorable way to make the vivid impression your teen or child is requiring. And all the other parents will say, "Why didn't I think of that?"

Try Both Natural and Logical Consequences

We have found that children from families who were more permissive or hands-off with discipline especially benefitted from logical consequences. Setting and carrying them out takes the parents from the buddy role into the parent role. It brings them off the sidelines and into the game.

Some children may learn responsibility and good choices better from natural consequences. Think about how your child learns.

Take, for example, a child who values good grades but sometimes procrastinates on projects. His parents are tempted to rescue him by finishing a project for him. However, if he needs to learn to plan ahead, a bad grade as the natural consequence will teach that lesson.

On the other hand, if that child is struggling to find the motivation for school work, the looming natural consequence (a prospective bad grade) may cause him to get discouraged and give up. This is where a logical consequence of "no TV and phone until your project is complete" provides some drive and inspiration.

In some families, dads tend to favor natural consequences (let's see what happens when you put your finger in that socket), and moms tend to use logical consequences. Try to vary your approach; if nothing else, it will keep your children off balance.

Fun for the Whole Family

Teach your children about both natural and logical consequences. Let them identify natural consequences in relevant situations.

For example, they can brainstorm the natural consequences of Tony's son skipping classes in eighth grade:

- He will get in trouble with teachers and administrators.
- He may have a harder time passing the class.
- He may miss information he needs later in life.
- He may lose the opportunity to take college qualifying classes.

Help them understand the difference between natural and logical. What are logical consequences for skipping classes that will teach and motivate him to go to class? The easiest logical consequence to imagine is usually taking away a prized electronic gadget. That result will sometimes fit the eight guidelines, but try to think of creative consequences. Your children can contribute imaginatively to this process.

We talk to many parents who work with their children to devise logical consequences. They tell us that it really helps their children develop cause-and-effect thinking. They also mention that their children's ideas for consequences are more arduous than the parents' ideas.

Other children may turn a conversation about logical consequences into a power struggle or argument, defeating the point of learning from consequences. In these cases, parents must make their decisions about consequences on their own and stand firm in applying them.

Parenting Tool #6, Following Through and Letting Consequences Work, is a great teacher for our children and young people. But watch out, another trap lurks, trying to sabotage the power of consequences in discipline. We'll neutralize that one in the next chapter.

Case Stories

Read each of the following case stories and mark which of the
Eight Guidelines for Setting Logical Consequences were violated.

Story 1: T.J. loves to play marbles with the kids down the street. Each time he plays, he gets down on his knees to take perfect aim. As a result, the dirt gets ground into the knees of his pants. After scrubbing the knees of his dress pants several weeks in a row, Mom finally got mad and told him to get into the washroom. She made T.J. scrub his pants. As he was scrubbing, she told him to get out and she would finish because he was too slow.

1	2	3	4
5	6	7	8

Story 2: Tanya likes to play hopscotch with her friend Alex. They drew a big hopscotch in the middle of the street and began to play. Pretty soon a car came down the road and honked to warn them to move. Tanya's mom came running from the house to see what happened. She reminded Tanya that she was not allowed to play in the street. She had the girls come inside to play for the rest of the day.

1	2	3	4
5	6	7	8

Story 3: Amanda is 16 and shares a small bathroom with her 17-year-old brother. Amanda has hair curlers, hair dryer, a curling iron, brushes, makeup and more. If she leaves all these things out on the cabinet, her brother has no room for his shaving supplies when he is trying to get ready. Amanda seems to always leave her things out, in spite of many reminders from her brother and Mom. Mom finally warned Amanda that if she left her things out again, she would not see any of those items for a week. The first day Amanda remembered to put everything neatly away, but the next day she left her stuff out all over the bathroom counter. Mom picked up Amanda's things and put them away for one week. Amanda was furious and promised she would remember to put them away next time. Mom did not give in. After one week, the things were returned to Amanda. Amanda remembered to always clean up her bathroom items after that.

1	2	3	4
5	6	7	8

Story 4: Katrina asked her parent if she could play outside with the other kids. They said she could, but told her if she wanted to go to a friend's house, she would have to get permission. After a while, Katrina's mom went to check, and Katrina was not with the children playing outside. One of the other girls said that Katrina went to Amy's house. Katrina's parents brought her home. They told her that she would not be able to have any special treats for a month because she disobeyed them.

1	2	3	4
5	6	7	8

What is the Logical Consequence?

1 Jenny likes to take her special porcelain doll outside and play with her in the sandbox. Her mom told her repeatedly not to take the doll outside, but she continues to do so.

2 Fourteen-year-old Angélica recently discovered makeup. It takes her twice as long to get dressed in the morning. She is more concerned with how her face, clothes and hair look than she is about being on time to catch the bus. She is often late.

3 José, five years old, loves to play in the mud. He walks through the kitchen to get water to make more mud, tracking it all over the freshly cleaned floor.

4 Josh is a very bright 12-year-old student. His favorite subject is science. He repeatedly does his experiments on the ping-pong table in the family room without putting plastic on the table. He also leaves his chemicals, tools, notebooks, and trash all over the family's ping-pong table.

Chapter 9

Parenting Tool #6: Following Through and Letting Consequences Work

Parenting Trap #6
Undermining Consequences / Rescuing

We now have discipline and consequences working for our families, but another trap lurks in the underbrush. This trap is the urge to bail our children out from natural or logical consequences, to restore the family to its previous operating system.

Our discipline is ineffective when we don't follow through. Lack of follow-through generates stress, power struggles, loss of control, and loss of confidence. If we don't follow through, how can our children respect us and gain the determination to likewise follow through on more important issues, like refraining from alcohol, drugs, and other risky behaviors?

However, by now we're almost home. We just need to operate Parenting Tool #6, the follow-through tool. When parents follow though, our consistency makes us authentic and credible. When we're consistent, our children can count on us. We become trustworthy and reliable.

> **When parents follow though, our consistency makes us authentic and credible. When we're consistent, our children can count on us.**

Following Through
with Consequences

Parents often talk to their children at length about their conduct or attitude, hoping it will change their behavior. When the reasoning doesn't seem to work, they also threaten to impose consequences unless behavior

> **Children don't usually respond to words unless they know the parent will take action. Children respond to action.**

changes. But how effective is that without a commitment to follow through?

Growing up, did you have friends who politely agreed to their parents' guidelines and instructions, but would then actually do the opposite? We had friends who would nod in agreement when their parents talked, but would then ignore all the talk and do whatever they wanted. They could get away with it because their parents didn't follow up and avoided using consequences.

Children don't usually respond to words unless they know the parent will take action. Children respond to action.

Does this Story
Sound Familiar?

In the middle of the afternoon, the children are sprawled on the family room couch watching television.

- At 3:00, Mom walks in and says, "You need to turn off the TV and get started on your homework."

- At 3:30, Mom walks by and asks, "Have you started your homework yet?"
- At 4:00, she notices that the television is still on. She states, "I will give you until 4:30, and then that's it. You better have started your homework by then!"
- At 5:30, Mom says, "Okay, now it's dinnertime, and you haven't even started on your homework. I've had it!"
- At 7:30, Mom throws up her hands in frustration and declares, "Just forget it! I don't care what you do. I'm tired of telling you over and over," and walks out of the room.

Has this ever happened at your house? What's wrong with this picture?

Parents in our leadership groups often say:

- There are no consequences for the children.
- There are no boundaries or accountability.
- The parent gives clear instruction, but does not take action: there is no "nevertheless" or "regardless," and no consequence is imposed.
- The parent leaves the choice to the children.
- The parent is not actually parenting at all, just giving herself a headache!

We'd add that even though administering consequences is difficult, nagging is even harder. We at least end up feeling positive about giving logical consequences, but nagging leaves us with an irksome feeling.

Learning Respect
and Responsibility

When children don't listen and don't take instructions seriously, they are learning that it is okay not to value others. Children need correction when they don't follow our instructions. It is critical to take action at this point so that our children learn responsibility and respect.

When we establish and maintain clear boundaries and when we back up our rules and expectations with consequences, children will learn to become considerate - laying the foundation for self-discipline as they do so.

Why is it so Difficult
to Follow Through?

Do you ever find it difficult to follow through on setting consequences for your child? Most of us do at one time or another! What are some of the reasons we have a hard time following through and enforcing consequences?

Our parents often say:

- We don't trust the consequence to do the job. For example, kids say they don't care or it won't work - and we accept that assertion rather than follow our own convictions.

- We chose a consequence we aren't prepared to impose - for example, leaving the grocery store if a child throws a tantrum.

- We are not willing to put up with the inconvenience of enforcing the consequence. For example, grounding your child from television might mean grounding yourself from it too.

- Thinking we can reason with them, we argue with our children and forget that we can't win.

- Sad faces, pouty lips, and big sad eyes on our children make us feel that we are being mean or hurting them. Instead, we are simply letting them manipulate us!

When we give in to the temptation to drop the ball on follow-through, we have given in to Parent Trap #6: Undermining Consequences / Rescuing. This deprives our children of the lesson the consequence is meant to teach.

No Follow-through Equals
Trump's Big Hole in the Ground

Without follow-through, all the good intentions of parents don't amount to much. Have you seen building projects that start out well, but didn't get completed? They start out with a plan, but without completion they end up as an eyesore.

Donald Trump heavily promoted an oceanfront condo project just south of San Diego in Baja. The first day of sales he sold 188 condos for $122 million. Buyers paid deposits of about $100,000 to $1,000,000 as 30% down payments.[1]

> **When parents develop the rhythm of following through, it starts feeling natural.**

Imagine the buyers' excitement as they invested in their dreams of luxury

---

[1] *Trump Baja Venture Leaves Buyers High and Dry,* Associated Press, March 7, 2009.
[2] Ibid

living on a beautiful coastline. However, in 2009 the dreams were destroyed when the project failed. Where did the millions in deposits go? The developer had spent them and didn't return a dollar of the deposits. What did the clients' millions of dollars of investment produce?

> *All that remains of Trump Baja is a highway billboard with a large photo of Donald Trump that advertises condos for sale. It hovers over a closed sales center and showroom, a paved parking lot, a big hole that cuts a wide swath, drainage pipes and construction equipment.[2]*

How would you like to invest your life savings into your dream and end up with a picture of Donald Trump and a big hole in the ground? With no follow-through, that was all the buyers were left with.

Follow Through!

Be the Parent:
Follow Through!

Follow-through is not only the key to real estate development, but is also the path to victory in sports. How many times have you watched the football bounce off a receiver's hands because he had already focused on his next move? He feels like a dufus. Then on the next pass, he concentrates on his follow-through and makes a catch that wins the game.

What's the key to a successful golf stroke? Golfers spend hours of practice developing their rhythm of following through on their swing. Take a look at the illustration "Be the Parent - Follow Through!"

When parents develop the rhythm of following through, it starts feeling natural, as well. The habit is formed, and it takes less effort. In the same way, when we follow through with consequences, the pattern is set, and it becomes easier to discipline consistently.

Our children's confidence soars after their disciplined study and practice result in great games, performances, and school work. So too, our confidence grows as we successfully follow through with discipline and consequences. We experience being "in the zone" as a parent with Parenting Tool #6: Following Through and Letting Consequences Work.

What's left to stand in the way? Falling for the buddy trap. This final trap is so important that we devoted the next chapter to it.

Chapter 10

Parenting Tool #7: Being the Parent, Not a Buddy

Advice from Kids in Jail

To introduce the final parenting trap, here's some counsel that teens once gave to their parents through Ann Landers' advice column. She interviewed a group of troubled youth who were in jail, and they made a top ten list: "Incarcerated Kids Write Rules for Parents to Follow."[1]

Waiting to start discipline until the children are older is like borrowing from a loan shark. Good luck making those payments!

The teens were asked what, if anything, their parents could have done to help them avoid the mistakes they made. Look at the illustration with their top ten list of parenting rules they wished their parents had followed ("Teens Tell Parents What They Need").

This top ten summarizes some of the parenting traps and tools in this book. What are your favorites from this list?

One of our favorites is #4 "Act like an adult, not a kid." When parents compete with their children for being accepted and cool, we think of Parenting Trap #7.

1 Keep your cool when things go wrong.

2 Don't do drugs and don't use pills or alcohol as crutches.

3 Don't cave in! You're the boss.

4 Act like an adult, not a kid.

5 Tell us God is alive. Show us the way.

6 Be tough. If we are doing something wrong, do something about it.

7 Discipline us, but love us.

8 Earn our respect. Follow through on what you say you'll do.

9 Tell us the truth, no matter what.

10 Let us know what we're doing right. Compliments and praise go a long way.

Parenting Trap #7
Falling for the Buddy Trap

We'll talk about the buddy trap and then the turbocharged buddy trap. The standard buddy trap occurs when our children are preschoolers or elementary students. We constantly hear stories of parents in the buddy trap. Examples include:

Companionship and bedtimes

- In so many schools we serve, teachers tell us how tired their students are. They can hardly stay awake in class. Why? Children stay up late watching TV or playing video games with their parents.

- Why is that happening? Parents are working long hours and then come home to crash. We don't always have time or energy to develop as many friendships as before, so our kids are filling that role. As a result, our kids - our buddies - stay up with us, far beyond their essential bedtimes.

Discipline and the buddy trap

- Who is going to give logical consequences to their buddies? Buddies watch each other's backs; they serve as the wingman; they don't hold each other accountable and create discipline. They try to avoid consequences - unless, of course, the consequences are funny. Are you remembering any stories of you and your friends?

- When parents get stuck in the buddy trap, they create a permissive parenting system. Their children then miss out on all the learning and development that occur through discipline and consequences.

Can you be both buddy and parent? In some ways, perhaps. We know many a parent of an elementary-age child who shows that it's possible to be strong in discipline and still feel that one's child is a close buddy. But when parents become buddies in the sense of being slack or permissive, neglecting discipline, the bills are about to come due. Their buddy is about to become a teenager!

Turbocharged Buddy Trap

What happens when parents have shortchanged discipline for their convenience and their child's approval when their son or daughter was in grade school? What are their options now, when their child reaches early adolescence and teenage?

- **Crack the whip.** Suddenly the permissive parent becomes a drill sergeant. Whiplash! What a disaster. The teens in this scenario usually rebel, right? Their wingman buddy parent has betrayed them.

Disciplining your child is like paying your bills. With consistent discipline across your child's stages of development, from toddler to teenager, you keep your bills paid. No late notices, no collection calls. By contrast, waiting to start discipline until the children are older is like borrowing from a loan shark. Good luck making those payments! If you fall behind, Big Tony knows where you live, and he has a bat. Not a good choice.

- **Fuggetaboutit.** That's Tony again, saying forget about it. Here the parent stays in the permissive style. However, the natural consequences of permissive parenting surface with great drama. When children are raised with little discipline, they miss out on vital learning experiences. They fail to develop the discernment they need. They are vulnerable to friends who take advantage of them.

Now the parent is in a battle with natural consequences. The consequences arise, and the parent usually rescues the teen or young adult from them. Over and over.

Parenting Tool #7:
Be the Parent Now

Parents have two choices: Be the parent now, and be the buddy later. Or, be the buddy now and the parent forever.

When parents discipline their children as they grow, their children gain the skills and confidence to become independent young adults. We usually think of that happening during college - the late teens and early twenties. Then parents enter into a friend relationship with their children that can continue throughout their lives together.

> **Parents have two choices: Be the parent now, and be the buddy later. Or, be the buddy now and the parent forever.**

However, when parents "loan shark it" by withholding discipline during children's early development and school years, the buddy relationship is short-lived. It ends after elementary school, and then their teens and young adult children struggle with independence. They lack the tools for independence, especially discernment

Parents Have Two Choices.

Be the buddy now and the parent forever.

When parents withhold discipline, their teens and young adult children often lack the tools for independence, especially discernment and knowing whom to trust.

- Therefore, parents may continually be called upon to intervene and rescue their young adult children.

or

Be the parent now and the buddy later.

When parents discipline their children as they grow, they gain the skills and confidence to become independent young adults.

- Therefore, confident, independent young adult children can be friends with their parents!

and knowing whom to trust. So parents are continually called upon to intervene and rescue. Have you known parents who were still parenting at this level into their old age?

All the parenting tools we've offered in the previous chapters help us to "Be the Parent" and avoid the buddy trap. This chapter will focus on how the family with positive discipline can make the adjustments to their children's needs during early adolescence and teenage with the "Six Adjustments for Parents of Teens." It will help us "Be the Parent" to our teens and avoid the turbocharged buddy trap.

Transition to Teenage – It's the Brain's Fault!

Parents often feel loss when their young adolescents morph into such different people. "How could you do this to me?" Thanks to advanced brain imaging techniques, we now know that it's the brain's fault. Your teen's brain undergoes extensive remodeling throughout adolescence that lasts into the mid-twenties.

Areas of the brain involved in planning and decision-making, including the prefrontal cortex - the cognitive or reasoning area of the brain important for controlling impulses and emotions - appear not yet to have reached adult dimension during the early twenties. The adolescent brain still is strengthening connections between its reasoning- and emotion-related regions.

> *Scientists believe these collective findings may indicate that cognitive control over high-risk behaviors is still maturing during adolescence, making teens more apt to take unwise risks in their associations and behavior.*[2]

Teens are able to perform at a world-class level in some functions including cognitive, athletic, and artistic. However, they have some key functions snatched from them just when they need them the most. As a result they terrify their parents with their vulnerabilities and risky behaviors. How often do you hear about a young sports hero or Olympic champion who thrills the world with a medal-winning performance but at the same time also makes tremendous errors in judgment: drunk driving, associating with criminals, etc.?

This is the very time that teens are becoming independent and want to go it alone. Still, parents need to simultaneously support that independence and also become more involved than ever during the teenage years.

Many parents attending our workshops are first-generation Americans from traditional societies. Their children are the first generation in their history to experience a Western-style adolescence. Essentially, they are the first teenagers in their culture's history. For the very first time parents hear comments like:

- Dad, you don't know anything anymore.
- You embarrass me.
- I don't need you.

Many of these parents take this criticism to heart and back away. However, when they experience our workshops and learn about the teen brain, they are tremendously relieved. They get involved with their teens again and let the critical comments fly over their heads. What do they learn about the teen brain?

Three Scary Teen Brain Facts (and One That's Fun)

1. The teen brain and the great PFC remodel

PFC - the prefrontal cortex. That's the executive center of the brain, the CEO of discernment and decision making. Dr. David Walsh, author of *Why Do They Act That Way?*, writes, "Its job is to think ahead to consequences and to control impulses that shoot out of other regions of the brain. Because it is still developing during adolescence, however, teens do not have the impulse control of adults."[3]

Teenage - what a terrible time for a brain remodeling. What could be worse than for the executive center to be on the fritz? After all, it connects cause to effect and enables us to think through to consequences. Therefore teens often lack the common sense they had when they were younger. Can you remember the endless number of dumb things you and your friends did in high school? David starts with this one:

> One of my friends borrowed his dad's car and took us car camping one weekend. We drove to the parking lot and walked to the campsite, right? No, because we were four teenagers with prefrontal cortexes in the shop for remodeling. So we drove through the fields and forest to the campsite. No problem with a Range Rover. Not so good with an old Cadillac.

> What natural consequences resulted? As you can imagine, the radiator was punctured. On the way home we had to stop every half mile to refill it. My friend's father was an Air Force colonel who wasn't too thrilled to see his car sent to the auto shop by his son whose brain was in the PFC shop.

We're going to suggest that parents need to step up their involvement with their teens. Even the smartest and most conscientious teens need parents to help out their prefrontal cortex while it's in the shop. Think back to your teen years, and you'll be both sympathetic toward your teen - and terrified! More than ever before, your teen needs you to provide love, clear expectations, and logical consequences.

By the way, the prefrontal cortex is the final part of the brain to finish redeveloping. Pace yourself, as your teens will need support in discernment all the way through their teen years and into their twenties.

2. The teen brain and emotion

The amygdalae - the emotional center of the brain. With the prefrontal cortex under construction, teens can't possibly also have their amygdalae in the shop too, right? Well, of course you know that they're both out of whack together.

During the amygdalae's changes, they cause young people to overly rely on "fight or flight" emotions. The brain can overestimate threat levels and overreact with supercharged responses. You may think of girls having changes in emotions, but boys experience the same. Dr. Walsh again:

> *The amygdalae also have receptors for testosterone, so in the midst of puberty, especially during a hormonal surge, the amygdalae are regularly overstimulated. As a result boys become emotional powder kegs.*[4]

Can you imagine the problems with communication these changes cause?

3. Failure to communicate: the PFC defers to the amygdalae

David Walsh cites two problems with the prefrontal cortex that cause chaos with parent/teen communication. First, the PFC misinterprets emotional signals from adults. It interprets many kinds of facial expressions, voice tone, and body language of adults as conveying anger, even when the adult is surprised or worried, not angry.[5]

Then, during the teen years the brain's executive center, the prefrontal cortex, defers to the brain's emotional center, the amygdalae. So teens often react with emotion rather than with discernment. During the brain's remodeling process, the PFC gradually regains control and finally takes over again.

What does this mean? Teens will frequently believe that you're mad at them and disappointed with them. They're likely to think you're scowling, yelling, and mad, when you're just saying, "How was your day?"

In the next section we'll suggest some adjustments that parents can make to express their real feelings more clearly. Get out your handy chart of emoticons, and hang on for a ride!

4. The teen brain and creativity

Good news. The fourth brain fact is fun, not scary. While teens endure challenges from a changing PFC and amygdalae, they also enjoy enhanced creativity. A teen's self-confidence suffers as the PFC goes south, but self-confidence can be restored through recognition received for exercising creative talents. This is the time for young people to pursue interests in the arts - music, theater, video production, writing, etc.

It's important for teens not to "veg out" during these years with electronic games and the like. Pursuing creative ventures and strutting their stuff in arts, athletics, academics, and leadership can give them the self-confidence to make it through these transitions constructively.

Good News for Parents of Teens

More good news - you already have practice! Your child experienced a very similar brain transition around age two. That may not sound like good news (you remember the terrific twos). But you've done this before, and you can do it again.

If your children are still toddlers, preschoolers, or of grade school age, remember that this is your dress rehearsal for parenting teenagers. This is the time to invest in discipline and positive parenting, while your children are still portable and happy.

> **If your children are still young, remember that this is your dress rehearsal for parenting teenagers.**

Six Adjustments for Parents of Teens

Parents, you're the leaders - so it's best if you take the lead by making some adjustments for the sake of your teens. What is the key point? Your teen sons and daughters didn't choose to ramp up their emotions or lose their powers of discernment; their brains did. It will be hard for them to override the interpretations their brains are giving them, but we can make some adjustments to help them.

Let's work with the issue of your teen's misperceptions of your feelings toward them. Your teen's brain says, "Dad's mad," "Mom's mad." We're the leaders in our homes; it's our job to make adjustments to the madness. Here are some adjustments we can make:

Parental Adjustment #1: Embrace Your Inner Goofy

We need to adjust to the perception that we're angry by demonstrating that we're not. How?

We're going to have to smile. A lot. We're going to look really goofy. But we have two choices.

1. We're either going to hear: "What? Why are you looking at me? Why are you smiling?" To which we can say, "I love you so much. I'm so proud of you." Over-the-top sappy, we know.

2. But consider the other option: "What!! Why are you staring at me! Why are you always mad at me?" Sound familiar?

We can lower barriers by portraying to our teens that we're not angry and disappointed with them but that we love them more than ever.

What stands in the way of following through with consequences?

- ## The Buddy Trap.
  We can get caught up
  in trying to please our children.

- Therefore we should ignore the popularity polls and give our children the gift of **positive, consistent discipline.**

- It is important to remember that our primary responsibility is to **"be the parent."**

Parental Adjustment #2: Reduce Your Intensity

Our teen's brain will interpret our nonverbals, facial expressions, and body language with far more intensity than we intend. So we have to make the adjustments. When you're having an accountability discussion with your teen, sit instead of stand. If you're famous for giving "the look," maybe talk in the car where you're sitting side by side instead of talking head-on, where your teen sees "the look."

In addition, teens' emotions insist that parents are "ganging up" on them. So in a serious discussion, it may be better for just one parent to have the discussion, not both. Remember how you felt when you were a teen.

Parental Adjustment #3: Say Goodbye to Being Cool

You're going to need to take a break from being cool. A six-year time-out. Dads, you're going to go from popular to just Pop.

You may go from

- World's Best Dad - first place trophy
- to Best Dad - Participant (like the trophy the last-place soccer team receives).

But don't throw out your World's Best Dad T-shirt or your Mother of the Year award yet. Your sons and daughters need you more than ever. Now you really will earn your stripes as World's Best Dad and Mother of the Year. But instead of needing you to be the cool parent, they need you to be the no-drama parent. Just like the story in the book *Love You Forever,* you're still expressing your love for them, just sometimes in more stealthy ways. Dads, you're doing just as much to support your kids, just without getting the credit. You're Special-Ops Dad now.

> **Our teen's brain will interpret our nonverbals, facial expressions, and body language with far more intensity than we intend. So we have to make the adjustments.**

There is another option: Keep having kids so that you always have a second-grader around who still thinks you're the greatest. (And keep them away from your teens.)

Parental Adjustment #4:
Parents Ignore the Polls

While teens are increasingly independent, they also really care about what people think. Who is more open to advice than teenagers? Why do advertisers especially target teens? They're processing guidance about fashion, dating, relationships, entertainment, alcohol, drugs, their future career, college. They're processing decisions about these issues while their brain's CEO is in the shop.

> **Teenage is the worst time for parents to back away and fade into the background.**

They are also dealing with more voices offering advice than at any life stage. Friends offer constant and instant advice through talking and texting. Teachers and mentors advise. Media advertisers target their every step. Somewhere in the mix lingers the faint voice of their parents.

This is no time for parents to fade into the background and try to sound like all the other voices. Our teens don't need us to mirror the guidance of peers and media. They need parents to provide solid support in processing the confusing, frustrating demands thrust upon them by peers, school, and culture. Parents need to be there for their teens by being rock-solid, not concerned about how we will be viewed by our teen's friends or by our teens themselves.

This is the time to "look not only to your own interests, but also to the interests of others" (Philippians 2:4). Which "others" need our dedication more than our teens?

Parental Adjustment #5:
It's Your Teens' Turn to Be on Stage

Remember that your teen's brain is providing great access to creativity. Although their creative expression may emerge in art, music, or comedy, teens' special ability to perform goes far beyond the recognized arts. They're on stage all day long. It's critical for teens to be interesting and entertaining to their friends. They amaze their friends with their humor and knowledge. Parents can bless their teens by being a good audience. It's their time to be on stage. Let them have center stage. Laugh at their humor. Don't compete - appreciate.

The old comedy teams all had a straight man: Lucy and Ricky, George Burns and Gracie Allen, Sonny and Cher. Guess what, parent: You were the funny guy before, but now you're Ricky, George, and Sonny. Your teenager will play off you to be the funny one. So again, embrace your inner Goofy. Don't take it personally. Just laugh and smile.

Parental Adjustment #6: Lose Any Put-Downs

You may think your teen is screening you out (all they hear is blah, blah, blah), but she hears every put-down. Remember that her peers are dishing out the disrespect and put-downs all day, and she's trying to cope with that. But home absolutely needs to be a safe zone, free from personal jibes and put-downs. Watch out for humor - you may intend a comment to be funny, but remember, you're the straight man, so you're in humor time-out.

A striking Scripture lasers in on this issue:

With the tongue we praise our Lord and Father, and with it we curse men, who have been made in God's likeness. Out of the same mouth come praise and cursing. My brothers, this should not be. (James 3:9-10)

The worksheets in Appendix 1 on Identity Destroyers, Identity Builders and Positive Power Words for Parents were written to apply this point. The words we speak as parents should always build up our children and never tear them down. As we approach the conclusion of this book, you can see that parents can elevate their level of discipline with no fear that they are somehow supporting their children less. To the contrary: as discipline increases, support increases. Out of the same mouth come only blessings that build up:

- Words that bless.
- High expectations.
- Positive discipline that builds security and belonging.

These are six adjustments to the teenage years that we suggest. What are some specific adjustments you need to make in your setting?

Positive Discipline
Protects Teens

We often ask parents, "What's something that is going well in your parenting?" We often hear a story repeated by parent after parent that summarizes this chapter:

> Parents tell of their teen asking permission to attend a party or event, and the parent says no. Their teen storms away and thunders, "You're so unfair." Often this demonstration takes place in front of their friends.

> Later their daughter or son reveals that they knew they shouldn't go. They actually didn't want to go but were pressured by friends. They simply needed and wanted their parent to say no. Many parents have told us that their teen hugged them when at last they told them their real feelings.

Positive discipline protects your children. It blesses them and builds them up. Parents who take charge with positive discipline are willing to be "the heavy" who take the blame for saying no in order to help their teen save face in front of their friends. You may not get that hug anytime soon, but we appreciate what you're doing. Thank you so much for your courage and dedication to your children by "Being the Parent."

---

[1] Adapted from *"Incarcerated Kids Write Rules for Parents to Follow"* Ann Landers column, April 1985.

[2] Society for Neuroscience, *The Adolescent Brain,* http://web.sfn.org/index.cfm?pagename=brainBriefings_Adolescent_brain, 2009.

[3] David Walsh, *Why Do They Act That Way?* (New York: Free Press, 2004), p. 44. Later quotations are from pages [[BLANK]] and 62.

[4] Ibid p. 62

[5] Ibid p. 78

Conclusion

Pushing Through Every Trap and Obstacle

What Would
Help Parents?

While we see that strategic parenting tools can overcome every trap, the parenting journey often feels like an obstacle course because of its ongoing challenges.

A national survey of parents asked the practical question, "What Would Help Parents?" What would you put on your list? The #1 answer parents in the survey gave was "Spending more time with my child."

What would help make that possible? The #2 answer in the survey was "More income security," followed by "A more flexible work schedule."[1]

How's that for a survey with unsurprising responses? We want to give our children more of our time, but work pressures and financial pressures get in the way.

Despite the obstacles, we find that parents are determined to become great parents. We lead a ministry that trains parent trainers. These trainers have led thousands of parents who are farm workers or packing plant workers through our parenting skills workshops. These parents leave home before dawn in the morning and work until dark in order to feed their families, yet they then come to our parenting training at night. They do that in order to become great parents and give their children a better life.

Parents continue to take on challenges like Marines attacking the obstacle course. In addition to financial and time pressures, parents battle a host of challenges that come against our children: negative media values, peer pressure, addictions, family disruption, learning disabilities, illness, and more.

Whatever obstacles you face, we know you're pressing ahead for your children.

Never Give Up -
The Hoyt Family Story

Our parent leadership workshops close with a video about Rick Hoyt and his father Dick Hoyt. At Rick's birth in 1962 the umbilical cord coiled around his neck and cut off oxygen to his brain. As a result, Rick was diagnosed as a spastic quadriplegic with cerebral palsy.[2]

Some experts told Dick and his wife, Judy, that there would be no hope for their child's development. Dick reports, "It's been a story of exclusion ever since he was born. When he was eight months old the doctors told us we should just put him away - he'd be a vegetable all his life, that sort of thing. Well, those doctors are not alive any more, but I would like them to be able to see Rick now."[3]

The couple brought their son home determined to raise him as normally as possible. Within five years, Rick had two younger brothers, and the Hoyts were convinced Rick was just as intelligent as his siblings. Dick remembers the struggle to get the local school authorities to agree: "Because he couldn't talk they thought he wouldn't be able to understand, but that wasn't true."[4] So Rick's parents taught him everything he would have learned in school, believing by faith that he was learning it.

> You are demonstrating your love for your children with every trap and obstacle you press through. As you invest in the positive discipline of your children, you are making vital, essential contributions to their moral and spiritual development.

When Rick was ten years old, a group of Tufts University engineers built an interactive computer that would allow Rick to write out his thought using the slight head movements that he could manage. A cursor would move across a screen filled with rows of letters, and when the cursor highlighted a letter that Rick wanted, he would click a switch with a head piece attached to his wheelchair.

The engineers set up Rick with the computer and instructed him on how to use it. The family waited to find out what Rick would say. They had expected perhaps "Hi, Mom" or "Hi, Dad". But on the screen Rick wrote "Go Bruins." The Boston Bruins were in the Stanley Cup finals that season, and his family realized he had been following the hockey games along with everyone else at home. They soon discovered that he had learned everything they had taught him, and had developed his own interests and passions.

The Hoyts' Extreme Journey in Sports

In 1975 Rick was finally admitted into a public school, where he enjoyed great success. Two years later, he told his father he wanted to participate in a five-mile benefit run for a local lacrosse player who had been paralyzed in an accident. Dick, far from being a long-distance runner, agreed to try it anyway by running while pushing Rick in his wheelchair. They finished next to last, but they felt they had achieved a victory. That night, Dick remembers, "Rick told us he just didn't feel handicapped when we were competing."[5]

Just as Rick's parents put everything into teaching him, Dick and Rick approached competing in sports with an extreme attitude. They have gone on to compete in more than 1000 endurance events, including 234 triathlons and 67 marathons. In a triathlon, Dick pulls Rick in a boat, then pedals a special two-seater bicycle, and then pushes Rick in his custom made running chair. In the Ironman Triathlon in Hawaii, they cover 2.4 rough water miles in the open ocean, 112 miles biking across steaming hot ground, and then run 26.2 miles, all without a break.

In 1992 they ran and biked across the USA in a 3735 miles journey that took 45 days. They have competed on some of the biggest stages in sports, including finishing the Ironman Triathlon in Hawaii six times and the Boston Marathon 27 times.

Rick's own accomplishments, quite apart from the duo's continuing athletic success, have included his graduation from Boston University. Rick now works at Boston College's computer laboratory helping to develop a system codenamed "Eagle Eyes," through which mechanical aids (like a powered wheelchair) could be controlled by a paralyzed person's eye movements, when linked up to a computer.[6]

You Never Know
What's Getting Through!

The Hoyt family's story reminds us to teach and coach our children as if they are learning everything! They just may be learning more than we realize. As parents, we refuse to back away from teaching, coaching, and training. Remember that a parent is like a personal trainer. Does the trainer stop providing instruction when the athlete is tired? Not a chance. Does the teacher give up when she receives blank stares? No way. In the same way, parents persevere.

"But one thing I do: Forgetting what is behind and straining toward what is ahead, I press on toward the goal to win the prize for which God has called me heavenward in Christ Jesus." Philippians 3:13-14.

This Scripture brings to mind the Hoyt family's experience. They pressed on by teaching their son, assuming he was brilliant. Then they crossed the finish line of more than 1000 races together. Should we believe in our children any less? Should we press forward with any less perseverance?

Despite the obstacles, you are continuing to build your parenting skills, skills that are blessing your children and someday their children. You are fulfilling the Malachi vision of turning the hearts of parents to their children, and the hearts of children to their parents.[7]

None of your investments in giving your children support and discipline are wasted - all of your efforts are valuable. You are demonstrating your love for your children with every trap and obstacle you press through. As you invest in the positive discipline of your children, you are making vital, essential contributions to their moral and spiritual development. You are empowering them for discipleship.

You are building up their sense of security, belonging, and value. We believe you are making the greatest investment you can make. Don't you agree? Therefore, we are grateful to you for all your commitment to your children!

[1] Eugene Roehlkepartain, Marc Mannes, Peter Scales, et al, *Building Strong Families 2004,* Minneapolis: Search Institute and YMCA of the USA, 2004.

[2] *About Team Hoyt,* on www.teamhoyt.com, 11/2/2009.

[3] David Tereschchuk, *Racing Towards Inclusion,* on www.teamhoyt.com, 7/1/2007.

[4] Ibid

[5] Ibid

[6] Ibid

[7] Malachi 4:5-6, Luke 1:17.

Appendix 1

Identity Destroyers

Yelling

Embarrassing or ridiculing

Ignoring; being too busy

Not listening

Comparing or showing favoritism

Using a harsh tone of voice

Too many rules; not enough rules

Lying; breaking promises

Overprotecting

Demanding perfection

Unreasonable expectations

Teasing

Parental fighting; making child take sides

Inconsistency; lack of trust

Critical; never seeing good

Conditional acceptance

Impatience

Neglecting a child's needs

Lack of sensitivity

Name-calling

Pretending to be perfect

Overreacting

Not respecting privacy

Falsely accusing; jumping to conclusions

Disciplining in front of others

Interrupting

Failing to discipline

Inflexibility

Not forgiving

Identity Builders

Say "I love you" every day,
and give
your child hugs!

Give children focused attention
rather than always multitasking.

Provide opportunities for your
children to explore their interests.

HUGS

Do special things with each
individual child.

Give your child choices.

Invite your child's opinions
and ideas.

CHOICES

Give your child a personal place
or space.

Listen to your child's feelings, and
honor those feelings.

LISTENING

Praise your child using descriptive
praise such as
"You are very creative";
"You are very athletic."

Let them teach you things
like technology, music,
dance steps and sports.

PRAISE

Identity Builders

HONOR

Tell your children how much you admire and respect them. Honor them in the presence of family and friends!

Give your child opportunities to help you and others.

DECISIONS

Allow your child to make decisions.

Share key responsibilities so they can learn, such as caring for pets, car care, vacation planning.

Accept your child's differences from you in temperament, personality, interests, abilities, and energy level.

PROMISES

Create traditions that you can share, such as camping, cooking specialty meals, and crafts.

Make promises that you can manage.

Allow your child to sometimes fail as well as succeed.

DIFFERENCES

Words for Listening Well

- Tell me more.
- That's interesting.
- How can I help?
- How do you feel about that?
- Please, thank you, good morning, etc. (extending courtesies to your children).
- Thank you for showing me how to do that (when your children give you computer tips, etc.).

Words for Encouraging

- You're really good at that.
- That's wonderful - how'd you do that?
- I am so proud of you!
- Way to go! I wish I could do that as well as you.
- I couldn't have done that without you.
- I'll love you forever; I'll like you for always.

Words that Affirm Character

- You're a very considerate person.
- Your hard work is really paying off.
- You really stick with the projects you start.
- You're a good conversationalist.
- You take care of animals so well.
- I can always count on you.

Words that Frame a Positive Future

- I think you're really going to enjoy college someday.
- You're really good at speaking & debating; you'll be good at forensics once you get to high school.
- You're very musical; you can enjoy playing that guitar your whole life.
- You're so good with math. That opens up so many career choices for you.

Appendix 2

About the Authors
and Illustrator

David Bunker and Patty Bunker are the authors and lead trainers of *Parenting Partners,* a system of positive parenting being used by parents and schools across North America. They lead a network of more than 1000 trainers who have brought tens of thousands of parents through parent leadership workshops.

These parents are raising thriving children with the positive, practical skills of Parenting Partners, including some of the skills in *Parental Guidance.* Parenting Partners teams are serving across the United States and Canada, and internationally.

David and Patty are parents of Daniel and Kaitlin. Daniel is a pastor at Northpointe Community Church in Fresno, California, where he leads the college ministry and also ministers to high school youth. Daniel is married to Whitney, who has a ministry to foster children and families. Together they lead missions trips with high school and college students. Kaitlin is a senior at Point Loma Nazarene University in San Diego, majoring in music.

More About David

David Bunker has led family-building ministries for more than twenty years. He served as youth pastor, then pastor in four California churches. As a pastor, David also directed Community Marriage Policy, an initiative of local churches to strengthen marriages and prevent family breakups.

David later served as co-founder and director of Project Home Again, a ministry connecting homeless families to churches. In Home Again, church teams and families worked together to find permanent homes and jobs. David led the training and management for Project Home Again in more than twenty-five cities for World Vision.

He was also a founding staff member of Care Fresno, a partnership of the Fresno Police Department and thirty churches that dramatically lowered crime in thirty of the highest crime neighborhoods in Fresno. David has also taught in the School of Education at Fresno Pacific University.

In 1995 David and Patty founded Family Leadership Inc., where David serves as Executive Director. He and Patty are co-authors of the *Parenting Partners* parent leadership training curriculum.

More About Patty

Patty Bunker has been a family trainer for twenty years. She became a California licensed Marriage Family Therapist after studying marriage and family ministry at Fuller Theological Seminary. As a therapist in private practice, Patty counsels parents, married couples, children, and teens. She also has focused on victims of crime.

Before starting her counseling practice, Patty worked as a high school counselor and as a hospital chaplain for adolescents and children.

Patty is a credentialed supervisor for counselors earning their graduate degrees and getting their counseling experience. She has served as adjunct professor at Mennonite Brethren Biblical Seminary and Fresno Pacific University.

Patty co-founded Family Leadership Inc. in 1995. As Training Director, she leads more than thirty training events annually across North America.

Ernie Hergenroeder

Ernie has been illustrating books since 1975. During his career he has illustrated more than 300 books. Still a kid at heart, his love for art, cartooning, and visual communications keeps his perception of story-telling fresh and alive with color and fun creations.

Appendix 3

About
Parenting Partners

Parenting Partners is an outreach to parents with workshops combining parenting and leadership skills. The eight workshops are presented by local outreach teams in schools, churches, and agencies. Parents learn to create positive and consistent discipline, structure, better family communication, and a strong home learning environment. Parenting Partners is a comprehensive, dynamic method for getting parents on board to become vital contributors to their children's academic success and character formation.

Our Parenting Partners staff trains and completely resources presentation teams to facilitate the program. Teams are serving in states and provinces across the United States and Canada, and in Mexico and South America. The teams are effective because parents trust local presenters and they love to participate in the interactive workshop sessions! Strong parent graduates then join the leadership team, making the program sustainable year after year.

All our curriculum, training and materials are in English, Spanish, and Hmong, with bilingual teams also presenting in more than a dozen other languages.

We are a national program bringing parents the best practices in youth development. One of our research partners, the Search Institute, has identified 40 Developmental Assets™ - the proven building blocks of successful youth - through their studies on more than two million youth. The 40 Assets are the real-life things our youth do that result in positive leadership, school success, and turning away from drugs & violence

Parenting Partners gives parents the skills to build these 40 Assets in their children.

For more information about starting your own Parenting Partners outreach team, please visit www.parentingpartners.com.